DATE			

Also by Guy Kettelhack

Sober and Free

Making Your Recovery Work for You

GUY KETTELHACK

A FIRESIDE BOOK

PUBLISHED BY SIMON & SCHUSTER

NEW YORK   LONDON   TORONTO   SYDNEY   TOKYO   SINGAPORE

F

FIRESIDE
Rockefeller Center
1230 Avenue of the Americas
New York, NY 10020

Copyright © 1996 by Guy Kettelhack
All rights reserved,
including the right of reproduction
in whole or in part in any form.

FIRESIDE and colophon are registered trademarks
of Simon & Schuster Inc.

Designed by Chris Welch
Manufactured in the United States of America

1   3   5   7   9   10   8   6   4   2

Library of Congress Cataloging-in-Publication Data
Kettelhack, Guy.
Sober and free : making your recovery work for you / Guy Kettelhack.
p. cm.   "A Fireside book."
Includes index.
1. Alcoholics—Rehabilitation—United States—Case studies.
2. Alcoholics—United States—Psychology—Case studies. I. Title.
HV5279.K4845 1996
616.86'103—dc20   95-24801   CIP
ISBN 0-684-81120-0

Contents

Acknowledgments

I thank, first of all, the hundreds of recovering addicts and alcoholics I've known over the past decade who've spoken to me about their sober lives and insights about sobriety. Thanks also to Peter H., my great friend, mentor, and cohort (one of us Huck, the other Tom, both wondering at each unnerving new adventure sobriety sends us down the river); Chris M., for his support, enthusiasm, and wealth of experience (and terrific stories); Lew S., for his intensity and insight and patience with me; Donna B., for her joy and endless receptivity; friend and former colleague Barbara B., who inadvertently pushed me off the diving board to start writing this book with a lunch date (lunch dates can be potent stuff).

Collective thanks to my colleagues and instructors at the Centers for Modern Psychoanalytic Studies in Boston and New York, who've unwittingly encouraged me to produce the first recovery book steeped in drive theory. Untold thanks to my psychoanalytic guide and dear friend, Reuven Closter, CSW, who, once again, as always, has offered me the space and encouragement to examine my own heart, helping me to insights that have informed my ability to hear the people whose voices fill this book.

Thanks to Judy Delaney, at Hazelden, who helped me to develop the idea for this wide-ranging approach to recovery; to my editor, Sheila Curry, for taking this ship on and sending it out of the harbor; to Connie Clausen, my agent, for her endless warmth, humor, support, and expertise.

And more thanks than I know how to express to Frank, who sees me through the steam of my fear and fallibility, and loves me anyway.

Chapter One

More Than You Bargained For

One morning, on my answering machine, I received a cryptic invitation from a tense male voice: "I need to talk to you about something, but I don't feel comfortable telling you about it on the phone. I know this is short notice, but could you meet me for lunch today?" The message was from Tom, a former colleague and friendly acquaintance I hadn't seen in three or four years. He gave me a time and place and a number to confirm. I quickly called and left a message to confirm the meeting with him. I was intrigued—and a little worried. Tom sounded more than tense; he sounded fed up, like he'd had about as much of something as he could take.

I'd worked with Tom on a book project several years back, and I remembered him as a perfectionist. He was detail oriented, quick to take offense, funny, and very smart. I worried even then that the pressures of book publishing might be too much for him: he always seemed to take everything that happened to him professionally too personally, and I wondered, as I prepared to meet him, if maybe those pressures hadn't proved to be too much after all.

Tom had chosen a surreal little restaurant in Chelsea, a Japanese-owned and -run Italian pasta place, the two cultures veering oddly but surprisingly pleasingly into each other, with meals that looked like Japanese paintings of Roman food (huge white plates framing tiny, centered piles of capellini topped with precise slivers of tomato, mushroom, garlic, and Parmesan cheese). The surreal atmosphere of the restaurant somehow matched my friend's mood and expression. His smile at seeing me instantly turned into an etched, baffled frown.

"Listen," he began after we'd exchanged some basics about what we'd each been doing in the past few years, "you've written all these"—he paused, shook his head, and gave the word exasperated emphasis—"*recovery* books, haven't you? I figure you know something about the subject. You're probably even some kind of guru by now, aren't you?" I assured him I was no such thing. The recovery book market had gone to hell. Alcoholics Anonymous (AA) was no longer the fashionable way to meet singles it had been a few years ago when *New York* magazine ran cover stories on "chic" Twelve-Step groups and there were many stories about celebrities going in and out of the Betty Ford Clinic. I was nobody's guru. But yes, I'd written about recovery; I was working on ten years of rewarding, if sometimes unnerving, sobriety myself; I'd talked to a lot of people to gather information and inspiration for my books; and I'd done a fair amount of thinking about what *recovery* meant. I asked him about what he wanted to know.

Tom sighed. He'd been involved with Linda for the past year and a half, and she was an AA junkie. She lived for meetings. Not only Alcoholics Anonymous but also Codependents Anonymous. She didn't seem capable of conversation that wasn't full of recovery slogans or jargon. Tom saw red every time he heard her use the words *dysfunctional* or *codependent*. He respected her—she'd been hooked on alcohol and barbiturates from her teens—and she now had had five years of sobriety. He knew that wasn't nothing. But she kept pushing all this "powerlessness" stuff at him, all this "turn it over to your higher power" Twelve-Step talk, something about the layers of an onion, slogans like "One day at a time" and "Keep it simple." Every argument they had—they'd been living with each other for almost a year now, and fights seemed to be increasing daily—became one more occasion for Linda's sermonizing about "taking responsibility for your own actions" or "keeping the focus on yourself." He loved her, he thought. "I mean, there's a kind of spirit and heart in her I've always been attracted to. But I feel like I'm in one long endless AA meeting from hell. 'AA comes before everything else,' she keeps saying. I'm starting to wish *I* came before something," Tom said.

He paused. "But it's not just a case of Linda's 'sobriety.' You don't know this, but when we worked together I was strung out pretty much every day on cocaine." A light went on for me: Tom's relentless "buzz" back in those days, his maniacal energy, his impatience and unpredictable angry outbursts, came into new focus. Having met many cocaine addicts since I worked with Tom, some still using, some in recovery, I could now put together a much more plausible picture of why Tom was as driven and uncomfortable as he'd been. "Three years ago I kicked it. I'd just hit a wall: I started to get so paranoid and so physically sick that I scared myself. I was bouncing off the ceiling. I wasn't only doing cocaine. To calm myself down, I'd pop Xanax like candy; I got the stuff free from somebody at work who swore by it as a panacea for anxiety. I started feeling like I was going to have seizures any minute. I really thought I was going to die. That's what got me to get help. I finally went to an outpatient clinic I read about on a subway poster. I didn't want to be locked up, but I knew I needed help, and I was ready at least to see some kind of therapist on a regular basis."

Tom was invited to go to some in-house Narcotics Anonymous (NA) and Cocaine Anonymous meetings at the clinic, but he got, he said, "absolutely nothing out of them. It just seemed like a lot of losers whining on and on to each other." He did, however, hit it off with a psychotherapist at the clinic to whom he was still going, on a twice-monthly basis, for therapy. "My therapist doesn't shove anything down my throat. She makes it seem like what I've done is *rational,* not some kind of divine lightning bolt showing me 'the light,' the way I hear so often from Twelve-Step people that they 'got the message.' I don't feel powerless. I don't believe in God. I don't believe that what I'm doing doesn't depend entirely on willpower and discipline—I think it does. I take a very pragmatic view of my recovery: I stopped because I was killing myself. I managed to change course because I convinced myself I had no choice but to change course. It was really a simple act of *logic.*"

Tom took a deep breath. "So why are Linda and I so at odds when we've both done the same thing—stopped drinking and using drugs? I don't understand. I only know that when I get to the point where I can't help groaning every time she says something about her 'higher power,' she explodes at me, tells me I'm 'in denial,' that if I don't start going to meetings and 'working the program,' I'm guaranteed to pick up coke again. She seems so damned sure of herself that I begin to wonder if she's right, maybe I *am* kidding myself. But then I'll talk to my therapist about these doubts, and it'll begin to get clear again that I seem to be doing what *I* need to do. But who's right? Linda or me? It seems like I'm always being forced to answer that question."

Now it was my turn to sigh. I'd gone through my own roller coaster in the past decade about program and recovery and what you needed to do to get and stay sober. I'd been grappling with many of the same questions that were eating at Tom. I knew there were no easy answers. The assumptions held by various experts or therapists who advocated one method of recovery over another simply didn't appear to be true. Dr. Arnold Washton, director of the Washton Institute, an outpatient clinic and recovery resource center in New York, reports in the book *Step Zero:* "Studies that have compared the results of all methods of addiction therapy indicate that there is no significant statistical difference among success rates of inpatient and outpatient rehabs or solely attending Twelve Step meetings."

Other evidence, Dr. Washton says, tells us that stopping without any formal therapeutic help is also possible: "A study of heroin addicts who managed to maintain abstinence over a long time—without any outside help such as Twelve Step programs or inpatient or outpatient treatment—does seem to indicate that you can, under certain circumstances, stop an addictive behavior on your own." This information can't help but jolt anybody with a recovery treatment agenda: the *same* percentage of addicts and alcoholics (by most other statistical accounts, a woefully low percentage) who stop drinking and drugging manage to *stay* stopped, *no matter what method of recovery they used*. It didn't matter whether they went to AA, NA, a rehab, an outpatient clinic; went into therapy; or simply did it on his or her own. No one method of "staying stopped" has yet proved to be more effective than any other.

So, in answer to Tom's question, Who's right? I could only speculate: "Maybe both of you are."

Two Conditions for Sobriety

What *was* it that enabled recovering addicts and alcoholics to stay stopped, through whatever means it took, once they put down drugs and alcohol? What are the "certain circumstances" Dr. Washton alludes to that enable some heroin addicts to kick the habit on their own? Were there, in fact, any common measures taken by *everyone* who stayed sober? I examined my own alcoholic and sober past, the experience of my friends, the thousands of stories I've been privileged to hear from the men and women whose "experience, strength, and hope" have filled my recovery books. There seemed to be two general requirements that popped up again and again, two conditions that had to be met before any kind of long-term sobriety was possible:

1. Breaking through isolation, realizing you're not alone
2. Getting support for your decision to stay sober

Certainly Twelve-Step programs have proved successful to many people in providing the means to meet both
of these conditions. But were there other ways to meet
them, too? Tom seemed to think there were. As I considered my friendships and contacts with other addicts and
alcoholics and the way they achieved sobriety, I realized
that Tom wasn't the only one.

What about spirituality? Wasn't that a crucial condition, too? According to AA, sobriety was an essentially
"spiritual" gift and could only be successfully maintained through an increased consciousness of a "higher
power." I myself have gone the AA route, written about
the immense rewards AA principles have given me along
with some of my most lasting friendships. I have written
passionately about my own experience of "seeing the
light": I had had what was inescapably a spiritual awakening on a late October night nearly ten years ago when
I realized, as if in an epiphany, that alcohol was killing
me physically, mentally, and—that word again—spiritually. But when I was honest with myself about my experience of this spirituality, I realized that my sense of it had
come entirely without my having beckoned it; it did not
flood in because of any conscious invitation or act of
will. I didn't "try" to be spiritual: spirituality seemed to
have taken care of itself. It didn't make real sense to label
it as a condition of sobriety. It had its own mysteries, motives, timetable, private and enigmatic manifestations.

I couldn't label spirituality a condition for sobriety, especially as I met sober people who told me flat out that it
wasn't a requirement for them. I could speculate—and
sometimes still do—that they just didn't like the word,
that something I would call spiritual had happened to
them nonetheless. But who was I to argue with them? I
didn't truly know anybody else's experience of sobriety

but my own. The two bedrock conditions for getting sober remained: I'm not alone; I need support. Even the least avowedly spiritual recovering addicts I knew agreed with me that these assertions made sense, that they were a part of what kept them away from a drink or a drug.

I still go to AA meetings today, and I'm fairly clear about what I love about them. First of all, they're often hilarious. Alcoholics in recovery are usually exquisitely sensitive to absurdity and the myriad ways we lie to ourselves about our real motives and what we're really doing. The denial that is the air we used to breathe (and sometimes still do breathe) colors everything: we overlooked, we *made* ourselves overlook, the most obvious ways we screwed up our lives. For me, an AA meeting encourages an astonishing, healing humility: there's no better place to appreciate how fallible I am. Past screwups, the stuff we did when we were drinking, aren't the only things discussed in AA. You also hear about the day-to-day grind today in our sober lives: getting into credit-card debt or owing back rent because you still haven't figured out how to handle money; lying sometimes to your lover or spouse about how you're really feeling, perhaps even having an affair on the side; railing against a job, boss, or colleague you hate or against the fact that you still can't seem to chart a work or career choice for yourself even in sobriety; dealing with grief, hatred, jealousy, or depression. "Stuff" happens—not just when we're high or drunk, but today, right now, in our sober lives. It's amazing, reassuring, and humbling to see a roomful of people who once got high or drunk at the least suggestion of discomfort talk with such searing candor about their struggle to deal with all of this inevitable "stuff" sober.

Which segues into the second reason I love meetings:

honesty. After an AA meeting, I can no longer lie to my-self quite as easily about the ways I continue to avoid looking at my life and the consequences of my actions. I almost *have* to be more responsible after an AA meeting. I've simply become too conscious. I also love meetings because they provide the two conditions I identified before as the bedrock of any recovery. They take care of themselves; they happen organically, just as a result of my walking into the room, sitting down, and listening: I don't feel alone, and I feel supported once again for how difficult it often is to get through a day *consciously*—sober.

However, in the past couple of years I've sometimes missed weeks of meetings at a time and wondered why I wasn't feeling terrible that I'd missed them. Hard-line AAers will give dire warnings about missing meetings: "Your disease is doing push-ups while you sleep, waiting to sabotage you. You have to be vigilant, keep going to meetings, and work your program, or you'll fall back into the abyss. And it'll be harder next time to climb out of it." These words once scared me. I knew how fragile I was; I knew how easy it would be to say "Screw it!" and go out for a bottle of vodka. But somehow, through the years, my daily resolve not to drink and my growing resolve to live as fully and as consciously as I could had sprouted strong roots. They fed on more than AA principles. What was the nature of this "more"? I reflected on my own halting progression through the past ten years of sobriety for an answer. What was really feeding, sustaining, *my* sobriety, my life? Why hadn't I picked up a drink in all this time?

Life Beyond AA: Charting My Own Course

I thought back to the first weeks of my sobriety, the amazing physical lift I'd experienced, which, as I listened to other people at the first AA meetings I went to, I realized was by no means a common gift. Some people couldn't sleep for days, weeks, months, without the soporific of alcohol or drugs or otherwise went through bad physical withdrawal. But enough people had experienced the relief I felt to make me realize I wasn't alone. Those first meetings were a godsend to me. I didn't really understand much of what I was hearing, but the slogans that Tom complained about, slogans that in my drinking days would have seemed like Romper Room nonsense, seemed incredibly apt and helpful. "One day at a time"—sometimes one *second* at a time. That's how life happened to you. That's all you ever had to deal with: what was going on right now. "First things first": how simple and clarifying this was! You did what you had to do right now. That's what you needed to focus on.

Words like *powerlessness, unmanageability,* and *surrender* had real meaning to me: I knew I was powerless over the effect of alcohol, that it took only one drink to put me right back on the slide downward; my life was nothing if not unmanageable once I was on this slide.

I bought what I read in AA's Big Book readily; the language seemed a little old-fashioned, but the wisdom of it rang out sonorously. I'd never felt comfortable being in a group in my life; I was a quintessential loner, an isolated asteroid out in space—that was an image I used again and again to describe the lonely desperation I'd always known. In AA, I began to feel a sense of belonging I had never felt before. I became a vociferous spokesperson at least for my own brand of sobriety; you couldn't shut me up. Not incidentally, my lifelong affliction of stuttering—alcohol for me was medication I used to "cure" my stuttering; it was the only way I knew of becoming fluent—began to lift in sobriety. Magically—again it seemed spiritually—I now could *speak*. In those first couple of years in AA, my hand waved wildly at every meeting. I was bursting with things to say, frustrated and resentful when I wasn't called on. I was like a baby who's just discovered words: I couldn't say enough of them. I suspect I was pretty obnoxious at meetings; I'm sure more than one attendee longed for me to shut up. But I wasn't going to shut up—ever.

Then something strange began to seep in. At first I had no word for it. Various adjectives suggested themselves: *ambitious* was one. Although I'd been content for my first couple of years in sobriety to do nothing but go to a morning AA meeting, go to work, come home, mash potatoes (a profoundly comforting "normal" act to me in those first months of sobriety—it made me feel like I was part of the human race), watch the evening news, go to another meeting, go to sleep, wake up, and start the comforting routine all over again, now I began to have *dreams*. I'd begun to want, even to ache, to live more fully. I wanted to travel. I wanted to write. I wanted to count for something in the world. I wanted to expand some horizons, build a life. It wasn't enough any more to be "a worker among workers." A cynical friend of mine in AA sometimes joked that he thought we ought to call ourselves *UA*: Underachievers Anonymous. "All anyone ever seems to want to do is go to meetings. Doesn't anybody here have a life?"

But AA expanded to include even this new ambitious me. I began to listen to other recovering people who did seem to me to have lives—rich, full lives. My circle of friends widened within the program. It was big enough to hold my growing doubts about some of the people I occasionally heard speak. They professed a rigid, dogmatic adherence to the Big Book as if it were a sacred text. My logical mind told me that nothing could have been further from what I understood to be AA cofounder Bill Wilson's initial intent: this was not a program of rigidity; it was crucially inclusive. Its terms, including that controversial "higher power," were terms we all had to define for ourselves for them to have any meaning. It seemed to me that any rigidly dogmatic sense of "The Right Way to Do Things" was at complete odds with the profoundly inclusive invitation Bill Wilson wanted AA to extend. You had to define the terms of the program for yourself if it was going to work.

For a while, all of my friends were "program" friends, and I was convinced (along with then Surgeon General Everett Koop) that everyone in the United States could benefit from one Twelve-Step program or another. In fact, my own repertoire of Twelve-Step programs began to include the occasional Alanon meeting and the more than occasional Sexual Compulsives Anonymous meeting. As my "ambition" began to nudge me, so had a number of what I was convinced were "character defects" (to use an AA step phrase)—most urgently, the urge to have promiscuous sex. As a gay man, I struggled with my own promiscuous past and my desire once again to connect sexually in the old ways. I could see this only as an affliction, a "defect" to be overcome: I sometimes cried at these Sexual Compulsives Anonymous meetings; I remember once throwing an empty coffee cup angrily across the room one night in frustration at not being able to "surrender" to the tyranny of my sexual urges. I had a lover with whom I was struggling to be monogamous. I struggled to believe that I only had to "let go and let God" to have the fierceness of my compulsive nature lift. That's what had happened with alcohol: surely it could happen in every compulsive aspect of the rest of my life.

These struggles merged with my desire to emerge and gave me my first passionate recovery topic for a book, a cry from the heart about gay men and compulsive behavior that I called *Easing the Ache* and offered (tremblingly) under a pseudonym. The joy of writing about recovery and about my own private experience of pain and illumination was in some ways simple: I was using what were once the most unspeakable parts of me—the compulsive, alcoholic, promiscuous gay man parts—and making them the *content* of my work. I was now broadcasting what I had once not dared to whisper (albeit, for the moment, under that pseudonym). I had managed to turn my own pain and shame into the stuff of revelation—not to mention a means of making a living.

Life. *This* was what had nagged at me two years into sobriety, the "thing" I couldn't put a name to. I got so much more than I bargained for when I got sober, much more than any simple notion of sobriety. By stages, the fecundity of life was revealing itself; old assumptions didn't always stand up. Certainly sobriety continued to be essential; in fact, it was the only absolute I knew. Nothing in my life—including breathing—could have happened without the key of sobriety. I had to stop drinking before I could start living. I knew this absolutely. It has opened a door that couldn't have opened without it. But beyond that door: *whoa* . . . Mama never told me it would be like this.

As I have gained ego strength, a sense of self replacing an earlier crippling self-loathing, as my self-esteem has improved and kept me more buoyant, I've been able to widen my field of vision and take in more of the world around me. This has resulted in certain slow, geological shifts in perspective. Traits I once reflexively labeled character defects are now aspects of myself I look at with more care and curiosity. In the more spacious air of sobriety, of consciousness, I don't automatically condemn, for example, what I once dismissed as sexual promiscuity. There's more to my sexual urge than I once was able to look at, there are more options of sexual behavior than I once dared believe there were. The world has now come to seem a vastly more abundant and mysterious place than I had ever imagined it was. And it is populated by an unimaginably diverse society of people who choose and follow an infinite spectrum of ways to enhance and cultivate their own growth.

Two years into sobriety, I expanded my own notion of cultivating growth. I made one important addition to, and in some ways a departure from, AA: I went into therapy, a fairly orthodox neo-Freudian analysis, which over the years has helped me to gain clarity and confidence in many unanticipated ways. Trying to make sense of the death of friends and my brother from AIDS, I even found myself exploring various occult theories and practices: I was and am riveted by different spiritual ideas of what the soul is, what happens after physical death, what karma we may be playing with in this particular physical incarnation. I'm now a shameless (if still often self-mocking) shuffler of tarot cards.

But somehow, over the years, the desperation of trying to "do things right" or searching for one simple answer or strategy to get through life has lifted, dissipated. I have more of a sense of humor about the fumbling ways human beings try to make sense of the whirlwinds in which they find themselves. I have fewer expectations, more curiosity. I have become sure about one thing besides the primacy of holding onto my sobriety: there was more to growth than AA. There were as many options to help me grow as I cared to open my eyes to see. They were options chosen by so many people around me. I didn't have a corner on the right way to grow or get sober. People, like a garden of exotic blooms, were growing wildly and wonderfully all around me, sometimes choosing very different climates and soil than I had chosen myself.

Some of these people are recovering addicts and alcoholics like me. Some of them, however, don't buy AA or NA or any of the other A's. Some who do occasionally go to meetings go for the frank reason that they like the camaraderie, not because they especially believe in all of the principles or steps. Some people, like Tom, never go to meetings at all: they find the support and encouragement they need in private one-on-one therapy. Some espouse rational recovery, a system that does not require a belief in a higher power. Many people I've met who have been able to stop drinking and drugging depend for support on a wide range of New Age "healers" and holistic health practices. Many recovering addicts and alcoholics both in and out of Twelve-Step programs who identify themselves as depressed depend on prescribed medications such as Prozac and Zoloft, usually (and it appears most successfully) in combination with some kind of regular, supportive therapy. And then there were the people who, basically like Tom, saw their addictive problem clearly and managed, without any evident formal help, to kick it and stay stopped, finding a sense of belonging and support in family or friends. Then, of course, there are the people I have known all along, peo-

ple for whom the Twelve Steps and program are an un-
ending source of help, comfort, reassurance. Not all AA
old-timers are rigid dogmatists: in fact, it's been my observation that the most successful (content as well as
sober) of them have developed a profound flexibility as
well as a sense of humor.

The point is, there is a much larger world of recovery
going on than I had any inkling of in my first years of sobriety. What characterizes "successful" recovery does,
from my now much wider observation, seem to devolve
into the two general conditions I've already identified:
not feeling alone and getting support. But the ways in
which we satisfy these conditions are legion. And none
of them, including the most ardent or orthodox adherence to the Big Book, can keep life from seeping, crash-
ing, thudding, or whooshing in. *Life,* in fact, is what
most of us hadn't bargained for when we made the decision to stay sober and received the gift of sobriety. The
pain of life is especially shocking now that we're not going to any lengths to escape it: despair, anger, disap-
pointment, boredom, confusion—all the devastating
human emotions that sent most of us fleeing to the escape hatches of drugs and alcohol do not magically go
away once we put down alcohol or drugs. But life, of
course, also includes joy—rewards of a subtlety, range,
and force to which we never had access when we were
blotting ourselves out with booze and drugs.

This book celebrates the diversity of ways we each find
to get through the day, to deal with life, to let in and cultivate new dreams and ambitions. We'll attend to several
broad but compelling areas in which life happens to us in
whatever version of sobriety we're pursuing: finding
support not only to enable us to get through the day
without chemical help, but to encourage and help us

meet our most cherished goals, to work on connecting with each other in friendship and love; learning that there is no one "it" to get in sobriety, that our feelings and experiences change as we change, and that we can learn to adapt even supposedly rigid Twelve-Step principles to our own lives, concentrating on what works for us, not on what doesn't; dealing with slips or relapses, learning that we can come back even after the third, fourth, or ninth try; dealing with food, sex, work, and other compulsions, looking at them with more compassion and curiosity and less automatic judgment; and, finally, cultivating the ability to *enjoy* ourselves, seeing sobriety not as a restrictive sentence, but as a means to become everything we want to become in our lives.

You will meet an inspiring, if sometimes bewildering, bunch of men and women in these pages, some of whom may strike you as outrageously provocative, way off the mainstream, some of whom are following an orthodox Twelve-Step route, many of whom have devised combinations of different approaches that they have discovered over time work to keep them sober and satisfied. You'll meet people with a few months of sobriety, others with two, five, ten, twenty years of sobriety, old, young, gay, straight, with many different backgrounds and assumptions. We are a diverse bunch, and we have so much to tell each other.

But you can depend on something singular: every person you'll meet in this book knows what despair is. Every person knows what it's like to live in the hell of addiction. No one here has chosen to recover out of some idle or vague wish to improve his or her general quality of life. Everyone here has chosen recovery because he or she was dying and wanted to stop dying, wanted to *live*. The voices you'll hear in this book give what I hope will be resoundingly positive evidence that, whatever means of staying sober you choose, the struggle to climb out and stay out of hell is more than worth it. You can choose to live abundantly right now. The only right way to do this is the way that works for you.

This book will encourage you to chart your *own* course to creating that full and conscious life.

Chapter Two

Do I Belong Here?

When my friend Tom let-'er-rip about his distaste for Twelve-Step jargon, I had the urge to defend it. This urge was fueled by the sadness and frustration I feel about the many people I've known who've fled AA entirely because of "program" language they found off-putting: words like *powerless, surrender, unmanageable, higher power, character defects.* It seemed to me that they were being put off by something essentially semantic and therefore superficial. AA words and phrases, I found, could be seen to have much larger and less judgment-laden meanings; they were more permissive and inclusive than they might at first appear. In any number of past conversations and in all of my recovery writing, I've appealed to anyone who dismissed Twelve-Step programs on the basis of objectionable words to try to find his or her own connection to the meanings behind them, not automatically to throw the baby out with the bath-water.

But after a few vain attempts to explain my more spacious and metaphoric take on AA language to Tom, I saw once again the wisdom of AA's nonevangelical stance: it's a program for people who want it, not for people who (we may think) might need or profit from it. Tom could not hear anything but "defeat" in the word *surrender;* he could not see that admitting your life was unmanageable (as the first of AA's Twelve Steps invites us to do) was anything but giving up the reins of responsibility, relinquishing what was to him an essential control. No matter that *surrender* to me simply meant seeing reality: when I say that I "surrendered" to my alcoholism, I'm really only saying that I let myself see what I was doing to myself; I acknowledged that drinking was killing me and I had to stop. *Surrender* has always meant to me letting go of the defensive and fearful evasive tactics I use to protect myself from (or blind myself to) an unpalatable truth; it means taking a profoundly deep breath and *looking* at the truth. Put in those terms, Tom could see what I meant by the word, but he was still put off by the defeatist connotations of it. And as for the "higher power" business, well, as we've already seen, he wasn't having any. No amount of interpretation from me was going to put a dent in *this* man's atheism.

Twelve-Step hard-liners tend to shake their heads sadly at resistance like Tom's: it's only a matter of time, they contend, before Tom sees the limits of his ability to control his cocaine addiction, his sobriety, his life, and he collapses from the effort—only to pick up cocaine again. But Tom hasn't collapsed. And neither have many, many other alcoholics and addicts I've talked to who have straddled the Twelve-Step fence and, at various times, come down on one side or the other but continued to hold to their resolve not to drink or drug. Not that it's a bad idea to turn the prism on AA jargon to see if you can make a personal and more visceral connection to deeper and more helpful meanings of the language. Why not try to get what you can out of a program that has demonstrably helped so many people? Actually, I discovered, from talking to recovering men and women, that people who are successfully sober, who have been able to keep from picking up a drink or a drug and sustain a basic contentment or satisfaction with their sober lives, do seem to make very idiosyncratic mixes of program and nonprogram sources of help. In the phrase many Twelve-Steppers use, they "take what they want and leave the rest."

However, there's a crippling problem faced in varying degrees by every recovering addict and alcoholic with whom I've spoken, and it has to do with self-doubt. Whether they depend on Twelve-Step approaches alone, mixed with other therapy, or on other recovery agendas altogether, an all too common worry for recovering addicts and alcoholics is that somehow they're not doing it right. Because "other people"—everyone from zealous Twelve-Steppers to equally vocal and enthusiastic advocates of nutritional or "rational" or other psychological and philosophical approaches to treating addiction—*are* so passionate about their particular agendas, often painting black-and-white models of success and failure, the unwary recoverer (and all of us are unwary at the beginning of recovery) often feels like there's a perfect way to recover of which he or she continually falls short.

This, to me, marks the real and most dangerous disease we face in recovery: the reflexive belief that if we don't adhere to someone else's standards of recovery, we're not doing it right. In AA terms, this may mean that you feel you haven't done a "perfect" fourth step (the step that invites you to take "a fearless moral inventory" of yourself). In nutritional terms, it may mean that you can't seem to stop overdosing on carbohydrates, which make you crave the simple sugars into which alcohol quickly converts. In rational recovery terms, it may mean that, despite all the work you're doing to change some basic illogical or self-destructive assumptions, you still can't seem to change the most fundamental ones that you've been told led you to pick up a drink or a drug.

As often as we may hear the reassuring AA slogan, "Progress, not perfection," our *experience* of recovery "authorities"—in or out of Twelve-Step programs—sometimes simply reinforce the idea that we're not making "progress": we're not following all the "rules." This belief that we're "not doing it right" makes many of us feel guilty, keeping what we think of as "recovery sins" to ourselves. This secrecy, this feeling that even though we're managing to stay sober we're somehow crucially lacking or internally flawed, sustains a self-doubt and even self-hate that are the most debilitating impediments we can have to our sobriety, to any kind of contentment in life. It's this internal feeling of failure that accounts for many people going back to drinking and drugging: "I'm constitutionally incapable of being the saint I'm supposed to be. Why should I keep pretending?" So we say, "Screw it" and go back to killing ourselves.

Let's see how a variety of recovering men and women I've talked to have grappled with these crippling feelings of self-doubt and have learned, however haltingly, to respect the particulars of what they each discovered was necessary to sustain their sobriety. Asking "Do I belong here?" doesn't mean you necessarily have to *leave* where

you are; it's just an invitation to look at what you're getting out of being where you are and to decide if you're
getting enough of what you need and want. The secret is
that everyone feels uncertain much, if not most, of the
time; ironically, acknowledging this (universally felt if
not expressed) doubt and uncertainty can unite us, bring
us together. *Doubt is normal.* The only bedrock decision
it seems wise to make is not to do anything to kill yourself.

Each person in this chapter and in this book has come,
often repeatedly, back to this bedrock when nothing else
seems sure. Where we all seem to decide we belong is on
the earth, alive. After making a pact with ourselves to keep
going, to keep breathing, to keep from killing ourselves
with booze or drugs, other choices can begin to emerge
more clearly. As one person who says he battles food,
drug, alcohol, *and* sex addictions puts it, "A good friend
of mine who has about ten years of sobriety once suggested something I find really helpful. He said, 'Work on
your addictions in the order in which they'll kill you.
Make a pact with yourself to *live,* then look around you
for what's going to give you the best support for the rest.' "

Learning to Lighten Up: Lessons from a Cat

Norma is sixty-two, and sometimes, she says, "I feel
every second of every year of my age—I regularly fall
into the exhausting trap of thinking that I keep the world
together and if I don't remain vigilant every conscious
moment of my life, everything in my and everybody
else's life will collapse." Norma laughs. "Then there are
times I feel about the age of the kids I teach—eighteen or

twenty—and want to blow everything to hell, leave my job, start out fresh, move to Tahiti, take on a succession of young native lovers. Which way I feel partly depends on humidity: when it's high, my arthritis kicks in and I *really* remember I'm sixty-two. At least, at the best times anyway, I can dredge up a sense of humor about these swings. In fact, maybe the biggest ongoing lesson of my sobriety—I've been sober for about four years—is that the only thing I can depend on is how I'm feeling now isn't how I'll be feeling in a while. The only constant I'm aware of is that things will change. That, and my certainty that Gordon's Gin is no longer a viable option."

Norma, who teaches English in a suburban community college, was careful to hide her excessive drinking from her friends, colleagues, various ex-husbands, and one grown daughter who only knew her, she thought, as "a standard of reliability: I was everybody's Rock of Gibraltar. If I told you I'd do something, you could count on me doing it perfectly and on time." She drank only at night, alone; she covered up her gray hangovers, her aching sick body, with Revlon and fierce determination. She assured herself that the outside world knew nothing about her nighttime drinking bouts and could only see the organized, efficient teacher she strove so hard to be during the day. However, one morning about four years ago, she learned she wasn't perceived quite that way by everyone. Someone had left an anonymous note in her school post office box that read: "You smell like a still. Why don't you go to AA?"

"I think the most horrible shock about getting this note was that I'd been found out. All of the lengths I'd gone to hide my drinking weren't enough. I didn't realize that even when I wasn't drinking, the alcohol was seeping through my pores. I didn't realize people could *smell* that I was an alcoholic. God, it was horrible—I was so ashamed." Norma felt more than ashamed. "I suddenly got paranoid, like someone had ripped me open, like everyone who met me could see through me." At first she dealt with it by going home early, calling in sick, and pouring herself a couple of glasses of straight gin. "But for some reason, this time, it wasn't helping. The anxiety wasn't lifting. I wasn't getting drunk—I was just getting *sick*. I couldn't drive out this horrible vision of myself as an exposed criminal, as someone whose rotten soul had finally been revealed. I started to fantasize about killing myself, going over different ways I could do it. I never got to sleep that night—for some reason I couldn't drink myself into oblivion. All I did, around dawn, was throw up. I called in sick later that morning. I simply sat at the kitchen table, unable to do anything, not even to drink any more—it made my stomach roll over even to look at the Gordon's gin bottle. I finally picked it up and hurled it into the garbage can so hard it shattered. I felt like I was shattering some part of myself, smashing it to pieces. Maybe I was."

Norma resolved at that moment not to drink anymore, but

It wasn't a relief. It just seemed like I was sentencing myself to prison, putting myself in some kind of deprivation tank now that I'd been "found out." I sank into a horrible depression, which lasted for the rest of that week. I didn't drink, but I hardly slept or ate either. All I could do was call in sick to the office every morning, pleading some kind of "stomach virus." What it really felt like was my *soul* had a virus. Although now I realize I was also going through some pretty bad physical withdrawal, too. The depression hit every part of me: I felt completely worthless. It even seemed too much trouble to kill myself. I didn't want to do *anything*. The phone rang more and more as the week went on; I let the answering machine absorb all of the increasingly anxious calls. It was amazing to me, in a sort of distant way, that anyone was calling to see how I was. I couldn't accept that anyone really cared about me, not even my daughter who called me back again and again. But one of the calls—I sat by the answering machine listening to each one as it came in—was from a student. She identified herself solemnly as the person who'd written that note. She apologized. She said she was just angry at me for destroying myself with booze. Her mother had died from alcoholism-induced cirrhosis of the liver, and she couldn't stand watching me on the road to doing the same thing to myself. She was a recovering alcoholic herself. She could identify another drunk, she said, a mile away. That's why she was so sure about me: I exhibited all the signs: the nervousness, the red eyes, not to mention, of course, the smell. She went to AA and found it had helped her. Did I want to go to a meeting?

Norma said she was too depressed even to be embarrassed by the student's call. The only thing that stuck with her was the repeated letter A: AA. "It sort of buzzed around in my head, creating simultaneous visions. It was like the grade I wasn't getting in life. Then it brought back Ray Milland and Susan Hayward film noir movies to me—films whose stars got tragically drunk and who then, at the verge of ruin and death, finally confessed publicly to all of their drunken sins. Then, in my mind, this student turned into my child, and I dimly realized that I might be hurting my daughter the way this student said her mother had hurt her. It was like a distant pang: I didn't cry; I wasn't *feeling* anything strongly enough to cry. I *thought* all this stuff more than felt it."

The student had left her phone number. Numb, wondering vaguely why she was taking the action, Norma found herself dialing it. In monosyllables, Norma said to the girl, yes, she guessed she did have a drinking problem and maybe going to an AA meeting might be a good idea.

I was talking and moving in a fog. Here I was admitting this terrible secret, something I'd striven all my life to hide, to a virtual stranger—someone who'd even written me a rude note! But I didn't care, and there was something immensely liberating about not caring. Deep depression has its strange cold comforts. It's like it chemically altered me—that's what it felt like anyway— and I just didn't give a damn about anything, about hiding anything: what did it matter? I sometimes think, in those first hours and days of my sobriety, that my body resorted to depression because it was trying to get me 'drunk' now that I wasn't giving it the alcohol on which it had learned to depend. Psychically I couldn't bear to face reality without a cushion, and the cushion, for a while, became depression.

Feeling like a zombie, Norma allowed herself to be picked up by the girl and taken to the basement of a church, where she attended her first AA meeting. "Nothing really sank in, except that there were all these people around who seemed so—I don't know—*awake*. I didn't have a clue what they were talking about. I didn't really listen. I sat at the back nursing a lousy cup of instant coffee and eating half of an Oreo. I asked my student to take me home the instant the meeting ended. She complied, we didn't talk much in the car, I thanked her when she got me home, and I walked back into my depression."

The next morning Norma did feel a little better, but she didn't know how much was the meeting she'd attended and how much was simply recovering from the physical withdrawal from alcohol she'd undergone the preceding week. But she'd pulled herself together enough to imagine going back to work and dutifully applied her old Revlon and some remaining vestige of the old determination. She went through the motions at work, dealt with her classes competently enough, answered questions about her health evasively but calmly. Then, abruptly, as she faced a long evening ahead of her at home without what she realized had been her best friend—"Gordon" in the shape of a gin bottle—she broke into a cold sweat. "I'd been numb for so long that I'd forgotten what it was like to *feel* anything. And this was terrible panic. I simply couldn't go home. I couldn't face being in my house alone." Norma remembered the address of the church basement and that they had meetings at seven-thirty every night. She drove to the church parking lot at six and simply sat in her car in the lot, waiting for the doors to open. "I couldn't think where else to go," she said.

This began a welcome period of going to AA meetings.

I listened and I identified with nearly everyone who spoke. I think it was the camaraderie I liked best, realizing that I wasn't alone in my feelings, my fears of being found out, my secret belief that I was rotten at the core and anyone who ever got to know the real me would be disgusted. A lot of people seemed to feel that way! The first, second, and third steps of AA: admitting I was powerless over alcohol and that my life had become unmanageable; believing that a Power greater than myself could bring me back to sanity; and making a decision to turn my will and life over to this Power were all, strangely, very easy for me to take and believe. It sort of reactivated an early childlike faith in some loving God, a white-bearded infinitely caring father in the sky, and it gave me something I didn't know I was hungering for— some reliable infinite source, something I could always depend on. But that was pretty much all I could take from AA—those first three steps. At first I told myself I resisted the rest of the steps because it was too early in my sobriety, I didn't understand them yet, and I'd come to understand them eventually as I grew in wisdom and my sobriety got stronger. But later, as the first year went on and grew into the second, I still found myself wondering about all this moral inventory stuff and making amends to people I'd hurt. Dutifully, like that child, I'd followed the AA suggestion to pick a *sponsor,* someone with more sobriety than I had with whom I could talk regularly about whatever struggles in sobriety I was having. I picked a younger woman who seemed to know everything about the program—she spoke frequently at meetings, seemed to have a lot of friends, quoted from the Big Book verbatim and with such love and enthusiasm—I couldn't imagine anyone setting a brighter example of recovery. I now realize I had picked the A student—looked for someone who seemed to be the smartest one in the class—so that I could emulate her and be the best, too.

Norma tried, she says, to

Be the best Twelve-Stepper in the world, but I kept resisting what I felt was a kind of coercion from my sponsor. She kept telling me I was ready to do a fourth step, to come up with that moral inventory. She repeated that it was only through these steps that I had the chance of maintaining my sobriety. She went further than that: she guaranteed I'd go back to drinking if I *didn't* "work the steps." She repeated 'Don't drink; go to meetings; do the steps' so often that I felt I was listening to a recording. Thank God, there were other people in AA I'd listen to who expressed feelings similar to the ones I was having at meetings and when I talked to them privately, feelings that sometimes a line was being shoved down everybody's throats. But I still had my first real crisis of faith, I suppose—it's like I began to doubt that this was a group to which I really belonged or wanted to belong. And yet, at the same time, I'd gotten so much out of my own version of AA: the idea of "turning it over," for example, that you take what actions you can and then let go of the results. This was profoundly healing to me. It encouraged me to pay attention to right now, the moment I was actually in. But, more and more, it seemed I had to *translate* everything I was hearing in AA. And, the longer I went to meetings, the more left out I started to feel as I saw other people speeding on through the steps and quoting Big Book stories like they were from the Bible. I began to feel the way I'd always felt when I drank and much further back as a child: alone, isolated, secretly going through something nobody else could truly understand, trying to act as if I believed what everyone else seemed to believe.

Norma pauses for a moment and smiles. "Then I got a cat." She corrects herself:

Actually, the cat got me. About six months ago, I looked out my back kitchen window and saw a baffled, wide-eyed kitten looking up at me, hanging precariously from his front claws off the windowsill. He was randomly black and white; he looked like he might have come from the generic section of a supermarket in a simple white box marked CAT in black letters. Nothing glamorous about him, he was just a normal cat, old enough to be athletic, but still a kitten, and a very loud, hungry one. He had no identifying collar—I'd never seen him before—and I can't imagine where he came from. No one I knew in the neighborhood had cats. But something in that wide-eyed kitten face caught me—I knew I wanted him. So I took him in. He adopted me right then and there; it was as if it were meant to be. He'd been looking for the right owner and it was preeminently clear to him that I was it.

The cat has been a revelation to Norma.

I'm not sure how to articulate it, but there was something in Gordie's total self-acceptance—yeah, I call him Gordie, in remembrance of my previous but far more lethal best friend, Gordon's Gin—that was riveting to me. It was like, whatever Gordie does, he does with his whole being and with an utter lack of self-consciousness. When Gordie is hungry, he looks for something to eat. When he wants to sleep—which is most of the time—he sleeps. He knows *how* to sleep better than any other creature I've ever seen; he has a genius for it. He *becomes* sleep: he curls up into an unutterably perfect picture of comfort; it's how everyone should look asleep. When Gordie is upset, he lets you know; when he's happy, he lets you know that, too. When he washes himself or tracks an unsuspecting bird in a tree, he is the picture of concentration: there is no more focused creature on earth. He is grace in action: everything he does makes instant sense, at least to him; nothing needs explanation or apology. He is the most entertainingly *selfish* creature I've ever seen. If he wants something, he does what he has to do to get it.

I'm not sure I can tell you exactly why watching Gordie has been so liberating to me, why it's triggered a new kind of self-acceptance in me. It's sort of that, when I see Gordie just be a cat, it gives me permission to be whoever I might be, too. I don't have to explain or apologize. I simply have to heed my own instincts—I guess I should say my own best instincts. What I mean is, I know that when fear and self-hatred motivate me, my instinct is to hide in the old ways, and I'm sensitive to what I've heard from other recovering alcoholics in AA who say when they listen to themselves, they're listening to crazy people. When I hate myself, which I sometimes—okay, *often*—still do, hating the fact that I'm getting older, that I'm not as pretty as I once was, that I haven't found the perfect mate and probably never will, I've learned to be very careful about my behavior. Anything I do that is motivated from that self-hate is going to be suspect, as I've found out over and over again. I always regret any action I take when it's motivated by self-hate, even if it isn't picking up a gin bottle. But I know now that you can sensitize yourself to your motives; I know when I'm operating from self-hate or self-acceptance. When I feel self-acceptance, I can trust my instincts, for the simple reason that I know at these times I'm not trying to escape myself, not trying to kill any part of myself. Gordie has taught me that in a way that Gordon's Gin never could. When you're true to, accepting of, who you are, you're in safe, fertile, wonderful territory. You can't really make a false move when you operate out of self-acceptance.

How this relates to Norma's perception of recovery and the role of AA in her life is only now becoming clear to her.

I've begun to realize that, despite the doubts and resistances I've felt to certain aspects of AA, AA has also taught me to *listen* in a much less judgmental way. I can sort of let things go into and through my mind without desperately grabbing onto them or expelling them in disgust. I don't have to be *threatened* by everything I hear. Again, Gordie is my role model. I look at him as he navigates his world and see him let the world be what it is, accepting what he is in it. Okay, I know he's a cat and I'm a human being and comparisons are limited. But he still teaches me: just "be," don't rush to "do" anything or defend yourself or feel guilty or really worry about anything other than what is staring you in the face right now. Trust your hungers and feel free to satisfy them consciously, but take care of yourself. Don't kill yourself. Have fun. I guess what this boils down to is a kind of positive flip side of that uncaring depression I talked about feeling in my first days of sobriety. That depression was liberating because it got me off the hook: if I didn't care about myself, what did it matter what happened to me? Now, I have a similar open-ended feeling of liberation, at least at the best times, but somehow it comes out of *caring* for myself—again, like Gordie so unselfconsciously cares for himself.

Now I go to AA meetings not to measure who I am against who everybody else is, but just to be where other people like me are, to listen to them talk about their own pain and their revelations. I now feel more like we're all on this leaky boat together, everybody is fallible, everybody is trying to get through the day in whatever ways they can without capsizing that boat. Some kind of help and peace comes from all this. I'm not intimidated by a lot of "A students": nobody hands out grades at a meeting. While I no longer have an official sponsor—I learned that I could exit relationships that weren't working for me, which is another big lesson—I do have friends I talk to. I no longer feel I've got to do the steps like some kind of fourth-grade homework assignment; I can think about them and adapt myself to them any way I want to. Nobody's making me do anything I don't want to do. I'm forging my own way. This helps me to get more, not less, from meetings. But it's also opened me up to other sources of comfort and help—friends outside the program, for example, who've got their own wisdom and experience to impart, even if they're not alcoholic. Frankly, I've got some wisdom, too, from my six decades of stumbling around on the planet. I'm not as stupid as I thought I was. The world seems larger now, in part because I'm not so afraid of it anymore, and I'm no longer trying so hard to fight or ignore it.

The Deeper Current

This larger sense of the world, of self-acceptance, of a freedom to move around and do what you want to do, describes an ideal liberation that most recovering people I've talked to do *not*, by a long stretch, feel all the time. Indeed, Norma readily admits her own lapses back to self-hate, which she identifies as her real disease, a disease behind the disease of her alcoholism. "All I can do is hold on until the storm passes—the storm of these terribly corrosive self-hating messages I still sometimes reflexively give myself. The one thing I've learned is that I don't have to act on these feelings. I can hold on, and they're guaranteed to pass. I wait until what I think of as a deeper current of life makes itself felt again—a current I'm most aware of when I'm not fighting who I am."

This deeper current of life is one for which Angela has searched angrily, assiduously, and until recently, completely in vain. She says she sometimes sees her life as two large before-and-after snapshots. The "before" picture is in lurid color: "I'm a sexy black mama, big beautiful breasts spilling out of a drop-dead black lace bra, otherwise naked except for my thigh-high skin-tight leather boots, lips wet and red and parted, sexy as hell, flaunting what I've got in front of a big foolish man on his knees in front of me, salivating, not *believing* how hot this lady in front of him is, pleading with me to come closer, while I tease and taunt him and make him nuts. Of course I'm whacked out of my mind on coke, Ecstasy, and a half a bottle of bourbon, but, damn, I'm hot, and I am in control, and it is a *hell* of a feeling." Angela exhales slowly. "Now the 'after' picture. It's in black-and-white. It's me with my husband and my three-year-old girl on my lap. I'm wearing oversized sweats for comfort and to hide my big fat body. No makeup. My husband looks down on me and our little girl, smiling, quiet, concerned, responsible. I hug my little girl, you can see I love her, but there's a sadness in my eyes, a trapped look. You can see it if you look close, and you know, as peaceful and sweet as this picture of a family is, something's wrong; you can see it in the mother's eyes. There's peace in this picture, but it's strained, and there's no color."

Angela stopped drinking and taking drugs after one particularly frightening episode when the drink and drugs nearly killed her. "I sometimes turned tricks—

worked as a freelance prostitute, that is, without a pimp—to make money to get high when I was in college. Men liked the fact that I was 'smart,' classy, a college co-ed or something. I liked the fact that I could get crazy—and drive *them* crazy. But it got messy. I went with some real creeps. After one particularly degrading scene, which I got through only on the strength of more quaaludes and more bourbon than I can remember consuming, I not only passed out—I fell into a coma. The guy I was with freaked, but—I found out later from a nurse in the hospital—he did apparently call 911 and get an ambulance to come and pick me up."

Angela had had some close calls before, but this one woke her up. "I didn't have a near-death experience or anything, but when I finally woke up—and there was considerable doubt that I *would* wake up—I was disgusted with how far down I'd gone. It wasn't just the prostitution—actually, I kind of liked the power that made me feel I had over men, or I wouldn't still be having that fantasy I talked about in the before picture. The bad part was the total dependence on anything I could swallow that would take me out of my head. Something snapped when I woke up in the hospital—I just knew I'd had enough. I didn't want to keep killing myself like that anymore."

The decision not to drink or drug did not, however, instantly translate into a wonderful new life. "For the first two years, I was still getting through school. I had so much compulsive energy, which I guess had always vented before in sex and getting high. I did manage to channel it into my work. In fact, I got some hot shit honors stuff done and a few scholarship offers from graduate schools to go on in my field"—Angela laughs—"which was clinical psychology, of all things.

God, if there's one thing I know nothing about, despite all the good grades I got in psych courses, it's how on *earth* this crazy mind of mine really works."

But for some reason Angela got cold feet about going on to graduate school. "I guess it was that old impostor syndrome people talk about. I feel like I'd bullshitted my way through school—through life, for that matter. I just froze. I was sure, somehow, I'd be found out, that I'd fall on my ass anywhere that made real demands of me. I just wasn't as smart as everyone thought I was." Angela thinks that's why she suddenly got married: "I was scared. I didn't believe I could make my own way in the world. I suddenly, desperately wanted to find someone who would give me security, take care of me. It was strange—one moment I was this smart, independent, sexy feminist; the next, I was a married, docile, and very soon pregnant wife. Something in me snapped again; I couldn't deal with the world alone. I needed—or I thought I needed—a 'daddy.' "

For a while it worked. "Maybe it was my version of what other people get from AA at the beginning. I never got anything out of AA the one or two times I went. But I did see all these people, especially the beginners, clinging so hard to whatever scrap of kindness they could find, chanting the slogans like little babies hum the lullabies they learned from their mothers. I just wanted to be told what to do, to be given rules, to be shown in some basic, concrete ways that somebody cared about me. I look back at the early days of my marriage like looking back at the earliest days of my childhood. It's in a fog, with my larger-than-life husband, all sorts of right-versus-wrong decisions to make, a child striving to be good." Angela frowns and looks confused. "Who *was* this do-gooder who came out of nowhere? All I know is, that's how I was then. I got pregnant two months after we married; by our first anniversary, we had a lively, squalling, and incredibly demanding baby daughter. And that's when the depression started to seep back in, that's when the feeling of being trapped really took hold, and that's when those lurid fantasies started haunting me."

Angela was able to use both her mother and her mother-in-law as baby-sitters for time she "just had to get out," time that, as the baby grew into a crawling and then toddling one, two-, and then three-year-old, got, as Angela now puts it, "out of hand." "I'd go back sometimes to this one out-of-the-way bar I used to work as a prostitute," Angela says. "I'd order a seltzer and sit at the end of the bar. No one recognized me—everyone I once knew had moved, gone off somewhere, or maybe just died, I don't know. Even the bartenders were different. But sometimes I just had to get back into the atmosphere of a bar. I no longer wanted to drink or take drugs, but I wanted something exciting, something to take me out of myself. I don't know exactly what I was looking for. As much as my fantasies are about sex, I don't think I even wanted to have sex with anyone. I just wanted a different kind of *attention* from someone. I wanted to be seen as something other than a mother, wife, and a might-have-been graduate student."

Angela would only stay a half hour, an hour at the most—"Bars are pretty boring when you don't drink," she said—and then scurry back home, saying she'd gone to a museum or for a walk in the park. But on one of her surreptitious trips to the bar, a man walked in with whom she used to "go out"—a man, Angela said, "who was, shall we say, *very* generous to me every time we had sex and also thought I was the reigning sex queen of the northeastern United States." Angela unbuttoned her blouse a little, hiked up her skirt, crossed her legs, and slowly turned around. "He looked like he would have fallen on his knees right then and there," Angela said. "It was incredibly intoxicating to me to see him *want* me so bad. Better than any drug high I ever had." The man asked her where she'd been. "Honey," she said enigmatically, "you don't wanna know. But where do you wanna go now?"

I couldn't believe it. I slipped effortlessly back into that old persona, the hot in-control whore. I barely gave a thought to my marriage and my child and the life I'd constructed for myself—at that moment, I would have gone anywhere with this guy. He got up from his stool, said what about our "usual" place, a by-the-hour flophouse hotel in the neighborhood, and I said, "Sure," but as I got off my own stool, something started to crawl around in my belly, this sick sort of nauseous feeling. It wasn't guilt so much, although I admit that my husband's and child's faces flashed in front of me for an instant. It was the sick memory of what it had been like to pass out in that flophouse hotel with any one of dozens of interchangeable men, the sick feeling not just from the drugs, but from the fact that this forced contact wasn't *satisfying* me—it just wasn't working. Okay, for a moment, I'd been able to get back to that "hot" fantasy aspect of my life back then through sheer hunger for something "different," but, now that I wasn't drugged up or drunk, I couldn't sustain the illusion. I stopped him before we got to the door. I mumbled something about how I'd forgotten an appointment and had to leave immediately. I fled him, I fled that bar. I heard him spit out something hoarse like "Bitch" as I ran out of the place. But I knew this wasn't going to work. I couldn't go back to that bar. I couldn't go back to the life I'd known. But I also didn't know if I could go back to my married life. Where *was* there to go anymore? Wildly I thought of calling up an old professor and asking if there were any way I could resuscitate one of those graduate school scholarship offers. I thought of changing my name, jumping on a plane for New Orleans, getting work as a waitress, reinventing myself. But nothing seemed possible. Nothing seemed satisfying.

Then I started to compose a suicide letter to the world in my head. That would be a way out—just step off this chaotic planet that kept demanding so much from me. It ran something like this: "I'm going to leave this planet anyway, so why not now? It's more than I can deal with, and I don't want to try anymore. I applaud everybody else on this planet for being able to meet its requirements. But I feel sick and depressed and unwilling to try anymore. I'm sorry. Maybe I will regret this in some spiritual way I can't fathom right now. Maybe I'm only responding to the triggers: struggling to be what everyone wants me to be (parents, lovers, husband, child, friends, landlord, the dry cleaner, the IRS), full of imploded rage and hurt and loneliness. I want it all to stop. That's all. I want it all to stop. Please forgive me. I am not throwing away your love, anyone who has loved me; I thank you for it. But it's not enough."

Angela shakes her head wearily.

It was somehow a relief just to admit, even if it was only to myself, that I was at the end of my rope. Something released in me a little, enabling me to walk home, face the only security I knew, even if it was stifling me. But as I walked home, I made a kind of new pact with myself: I wasn't going to be silent about this pain. I was going to find a way to *say* it. It's funny, all the reading I'd done in Freud about the "talking cure"—I guess I was never sure if talking could be a cure, but it did seem like a nice idea to spill everything out to *somebody*. I found myself remembering how I felt when I decided not to go to that hotel with that man at the bar, not so much guilty as sick of all of that not *working*. It was like I began to let up on myself, not dividing myself so neatly between whore and saint. I had the first inkling that these whore and saint elements were equally a part of me and needed equal attention. I had to find a way to give them that attention. That's all I knew then.

This feeling of wanting to break the silence led Angela eventually into therapy with an avowedly feminist but married-with-children analyst, who, Angela says,

Is a kind of Teflon role model for me. What I mean is, she won't let me stick to her. She keeps sort of holding up a mirror so that I can see myself, get back to my own feelings and thoughts and—what's the trendy way to put it?—"own" them. I realized that as a whore, as a graduate student, as a mother, as a wife, I'd thought I had to become each of those roles. I regularly kept losing myself in them and then struggling against their confines when I realized I couldn't *only* be the role. This is all in the beginning stages—I've only really had these thoughts recently. At first I wanted to spill everything out to my husband, including my trips to the bar and almost going home with that man, but I kept the lid on that. It was important for me to get this stuff out, but not to him. It would only have hurt him needlessly. My therapist is a lifeline for me—I really am trying to tell her everything. But the funny thing that keeps happening when I pull on that lifeline, pull it to me with all the desperation of a drowning woman, what I find on the other end of it is not my therapist, I find myself. And I don't drown. I keep proving to myself that I can keep going.

How this nascent revelation relates to sobriety is almost, for Angela, beside the point.

Sobriety isn't a term I use very much. At least, I don't just see my life in terms of "before I drank" and "after I drank," the way I got the idea people in AA do. There are a lot of befores and afters in my life. Before my father died, after he died. Before I got into prostitution, after I got into it. Before I drank and drugged, after I drank and drugged. School, marriage, motherhood—all of these were before-and-after rites of passage. They *all* were important. I didn't suddenly learn "everything" when I stopped drinking and drugging, and I also didn't know nothing *while* I was drinking and drugging. In fact, I learned a lot about human nature in those years! It's not this black-and-white thing anymore. So yes, I guess I call myself sober, but I also call myself a lot of other things, mostly right now a confused black woman who wants to get on with her life and who's damned if she's not going to try to get the best she can out of it. Now I'm starting to see whatever desire to emerge I ever had not as something dangerous, not as something that requires me to junk everything I'm doing and reinvent myself as somebody totally different, but as a kind of cry from my soul to be heard and seen as who I am and to be as fully conscious as possible. I don't have to react in that old, baby-like, frustrated "blow-it-all-to-hell" way. I can be a lot of different feelings and things and beliefs at once. And recently I've tapped into a whole new sense of satisfaction, a kind of unbroken, more subtle current beneath everything, which gives me a sense of *pleasure,* really, in seeing life unfold, a satisfaction that is deeper than the transitory thrills I knew when I was high and acting out—or sober and acting out.

Like Norma, Angela doesn't claim she feels this "current" all the time. "Far from it," she says. "But I can get back to it—even in the midst of my shrieking daughter throwing her oatmeal at me. It's—I don't know—sort of like a sense of *humor* that's always there. That's what was always missing in any of my previous incarnations. Humor. Acceptance. And the willingness to keep my eyes open and take the next step."

"I'm Not Going Away . . ."

Len goes to AA religiously. "I don't see how anyone can keep sober without it," he says, "although all that really means is, I don't see how *I* could keep sober without it." Len has quite a drinking history, including frequent dry-outs in rehabs and jails, (mostly) petty thievery, a lot of living on the streets, and now, he says, "Waddya know? I've got AIDS. Surprised? I'm sure as hell not." At forty-six, Len's T cells are down to zero, but so far the only opportunistic infection he's had to deal with is the purple skin blotches of Kaposi's sarcoma, which, he says, "is mostly under control. Although lately I do keep getting other strange outbreaks on my skin, these weird, sometimes-itchy, sometimes-not rashes. I'm one of my hospital dermatology clinic's prize specimens, it seems to me; they keep bringing in medical students to study what new peculiar irruption has blossomed out on my skin. I can't help thinking of it as a symbol, somehow—it's like all of the stuff I don't understand about myself keeps seeping out my pores. And it requires constant, daily maintenance. Just like my sobriety."

Len says he probably got AIDS from this or that shared needle, although, at various points in the past, he'd allow himself to be "serviced" in this or that down-and-out porno movie for "chump change"; he did anything he had to to keep drinking and getting the odd hit of heroin. "So maybe it was sex. I was too passed out most of the time to let you know who I screwed or got screwed by. I'm not gay, but my body was pretty much open territory for anyone who wanted it, especially anyone who could get me high. And when I was younger, I wasn't so bad looking. So . . ."

Len did marry early on and has a twenty-one-year-old son who looks him up from time to time.

It's strange—I was more than just your average absent father. I mean, I was half dead most of the time. But now that I'm sober and now that it looks like I don't exactly have decades of life ahead of me, I've found myself feeling love for this son that I didn't know I had in me. We do stuff together now, go to baseball games, sometimes a museum. He's quiet, brought up in a foster home after his mother died, goes to the state university, and wants to be a metallurgical engineer, of all things. God, I can hardly pronounce it! I'm so proud of him. I can't believe I had anything to do with bringing him into the world. And sure, I guess I can't help living through him a little bit. It's like he's the good side of me. But mostly, I'm bowled over by how much love I feel for him. It's like it was backed up all those years, and now it has someplace to come out.

Once Len accepted his alcoholism—which, he says, meant "accepting that I wanted to live, not die,"—he has followed the completely straight-and-narrow AA path.

I didn't know shit when I came into the rooms. I got myself a sponsor, a real hard-nosed guy who basically *told* me I didn't know shit and that I had to memorize, line by line, every word in the definition of the first step in Bill Wilson's Big Book every night and report to him what I'd memorized the next day. He was like a general from hell. But I'd drunk and drugged so heavily for so long, it took something that forceful to get me to listen. He made me call him three, four times a day. He made me go to three, four meetings a day. He made me talk about what I'd heard in the meetings. He told me flat out when he thought I was spouting b.s.—especially when I started to feel sorry for myself. And yet, he wouldn't go away. He was just there for me all the time. It was tough love, I guess. I'd never experienced anyone who simply *stayed with me* the way he did. He was demonstrating his love, not talking about it. I went through every step, studied every AA tradition, got myself making coffee at one meeting, cleaning up and setting up chairs at another. It's been the whole structure of my life. And I haven't drunk or drugged for five years, which, believe me, is a miracle.

An interesting turning point happened for Len when his sponsor required him to take on a sponsee—someone, Len said, who was as full of shit as Len was when he first came into the rooms. Len dutifully volunteered at one of his meetings to act as sponsor for anyone new, expecting some Bowery bum like himself to take him up on the offer. He was planning all sorts of military-style strategy with any new "Len," almost looking forward to it: "I liked the idea that the tables had turned, and that I might be able to talk some sense into someone else for a change." But, he said, "this skinny, early-twenties punk kid walked up to me at the end of the meeting and said he wanted to try me out." Len had never met anyone like this guy, Rick. "It certainly wasn't a version of me walking up. I mean, even though I have AIDS, I'm not wasting away yet. I'm still about two hundred twenty pounds, six foot. Rick must be about one hundred twenty-five pounds, five feet six inches or something. This little sullen stick of a thing. Rick told me right off he suspected AA was full of shit, but I looked harmless enough, and he thought he'd at least try a little of the orthodox route before trashing the whole program. He did sort of like listening to people at meetings. And he thought he might meet a hot woman at one of these places. He'd gotten sick of the whacked-out girls he'd been hanging with before."

Len said he was bewildered by this punk-rock kid but even more bewildered by his own reluctance to play sergeant general with him.

I don't know—there was something about Rick's arrogance that struck a chord in me. I just wanted to listen to him for a while, to see what was going on in him. I won't even say I especially wanted to help him or change him or anything like that. I guess I sensed something beneath all that arrogance. Like he really needed to dump something bad. I knew what that felt like. And I guess, with my own son being about Rick's age, I couldn't help making some comparisons. Somehow my son had turned out all right—I don't mean turned into a 'good' boy especially. He just didn't seem as tortured as Rick did, as I was when I was Rick's age. So in our first 'conversations' over coffee in a nearby greasy diner, which were really more monologues from Rick, I pretty much kept my mouth shut. Rick seemed to be surprised by that at first and then just to accept it, and he kept on talking.

Rick rambled unpredictably about some early childhood memories as a spoiled kid of a divorced mother, a lot of money, a bunch of private schools that threw him out for doing drugs, getting into fights, once getting a girl pregnant, some trips to Europe he can barely remember because he was so stoned on grass, a lot of trips to various shrinks who basically didn't know what to do with him, one expensive psychiatric institution his mother got him into from which he escaped, a couple of "art band" experiences that basically required him to scream half naked on various smoky downtown stages, pounding away maniacally at some untuned electrical guitar, after which, if he wasn't impotent from all the drugs and booze, came various obligatory attempts to screw whatever band groupies happened to be hanging around that night. In some ways, it was, Len said,

like a tired script from some misunderstood-teenager TV movie, except for the look in Rick's eyes while he went on and on. It was like, he started out in what he must have thought was a "cool" monotone, but the more details he told me, the more urgently he spoke and looked at me, not just for approval, maybe not for approval at all, but to see if I was *hearing* him. I think it freaked him out a little that I wasn't saying much back. I wasn't giving him the conventional shocked responses that maybe he thought an older guy was supposed to give him about all his drugged-out weird sexual scenarios. I'd been through my own version of this circus, which maybe I'd let Rick know at some point. But my instinct told me to shut up and just let him talk and let him see by the fact that I wasn't turning my eyes away from him, that I wasn't grossed out by any of the sordid details, that I simply was going to *stay*. And I started to realize that *that* was what had worked for me as much as anything else with my own sponsor at the beginning. It wasn't memorizing the steps or doing all that AA stuff that was most important. It was letting me know that he wasn't going to go away. He proved that to me, moment by moment, day by day. He demonstrated that he could withstand anything I told him, that it wouldn't turn him against me.

This idea didn't seem like much of a revelation at the time, Len said, but it's grown into one.

Rick is having a lot harder time with the Twelve Steps and all of the stuff I had no trouble swallowing whole. Frankly, I don't know whether he's going to stay in AA. But I suspect he'll stay talking to me, at least for as long as either one of us is around. I do tell him what I've gotten out of the program, and now I don't shut up as much when he speaks. I've learned from my own sponsor to develop a pretty good crap detector, and I let Rick know when I think he's kidding himself. But I'm not a sergeant general about it. *I* needed a sergeant general, but not everybody else does. The one thing I realize from all of this, though, is that working with Rick is helping to keep me sober. It's giving me a real sense of getting through to somebody—of human contact, I guess—more of which I get from my sponsor and my son and friends in the program. Now that the length of my life has been called into severe question, I can't help seeing life as one tiny instant at a time. I don't know how to say it more clearly: the only moment we've got is *now.* AA absolutely works for me, but the main gift I get out of it, which Rick and my sponsor have really taught me, is that there *is* love you can reach out for, get, give, depend on. What happens to Rick or me or anyone else a minute from now is a crap game, but we can sure as hell be conscious of what's happening right now—and maybe even enjoy it. Who the hell knows what's going to happen next? The only thing I know is that I have the choice not to be drunk when it does.

In common with every recovering alcoholic and addict I've met and listened to, Norma, Angela, Len, and Rick each went through a sometimes terrifying, sometimes numbing initial period of needing guidance when they first stopped drinking and drugging. Sometimes AA provided this guidance, sometimes a spouse did, sometimes a therapist, sometimes a friend. When we first get sober, many of us require emergency room attention: triage; on-the-spot, stop-the-bleeding care. But as our bodies and psyches begin to heal, as we discover we can withstand the force of sober, or conscious, life, we start—sometimes very much without wanting or expecting it—to grow. Unhealed wounds meshed with or separate from alcoholism or drug addiction make themselves felt again. The various exigencies of our lives, the various mix of nature-and-nurture that makes us uniquely ourselves, start to flow again, stirring us, confusing us, motivating us.

It's frightening to grow; we're always becoming something we've never been before. Many learn to hang on through this fear, to develop various on-the-spot strategies that *fit* whatever fresh pain or joy or insight was thrust upon them. Norma has learned the difference between how self-hate and self-acceptance *feel:* she's now alert to when she can trust her instincts and when she can't. It's a moment-by-moment test for her: does she want to escape life because she loathes who she is? Or does she want to embrace it, or at least tolerate it, because she knows she's basically all right? Angela has learned that she can be—in fact, *is*—many different traits, feelings, aspects of personality. Slowly, she's developing a sense of self that, like Norma's growing sense of self, can contain all of who she is—a self she doesn't have to fear, hate, change, or run from. She's also detected the presence of a deeper satisfaction beneath all of the turmoil of personality and desires and seeming contradictions at the surface of her life, a deeper current that she's learning will not go away, that she can tap into even at the most chaotic moments. Len has similarly discovered this greater stability of self. It has come for him via a kind of mirror revelation, as he discovered, first with his sponsor, then through his own choice to "stay" with his son and his sponsee, that there is an abundant, unstoppable source of love and help available to him. Rick is just at the beginning of seeing that he can be who he is, that nothing he's done sober or high is enough to block the possibility of being heard, accepted, and possibly even loved.

As varied as each of their routes is, Norma, Angela, Len, and Rick are each discovering something similar: that they can tolerate being in their own skin sober. There is life beyond the first bewildering blast of consciousness they experienced once they stopped getting high. The good news is that there is subtler and deeper healing beyond the triage of the emergency-room state of early sobriety. The less pleasant news is that the route to this subtler, deeper healing is rarely as smooth and Zenlike as we may wish. There are a lot of unnerving, if barely visible, bumps in the road ahead to look out for.

Chapter Three

Getting a Life

It's bewildering to be sober when your world was once organized to help you reach one goal and one goal only: getting high. Even years into sobriety, our expectations often still reflect the get-high-you-deserve-it dynamics of our former lives. Drugs and alcohol were often the ways we rewarded ourselves or medicated ourselves at the end of any day (or hour or minute) we felt we couldn't deal with consciously. It's very common to hold onto this idea of a simplistic reward system even in recovery. We may think, I've been the best little boy/girl in the world. I'm following all the rules, doing everything right. Where's my prize? Where's my new bicycle, job, lover, home, car, body, wisdom?

Bicycles don't always come on cue. And when we discover that they don't, we may feel duped. What's the point of getting sober if it doesn't get you the happiness and success you've defined for yourself? Worse, you look around and see other people who are most decidedly *not* playing by "the rules"—people who may even be drinking and drugging—and they're getting the bicycle, job, lover, home, car, body, wisdom, *you* want. How is this possible? How can they get away with all that and still "succeed"?

Feelings of frustration and disgruntlement run a lot deeper and crop up a lot more frequently in recovering people's lives than is ever fully admitted or reported. Because we don't realize how common these feelings are, a lot of us continue to think we're uniquely maladaptive, we're still doing it (work, love, recovery, life) "wrong." Sobriety may even ultimately seem more of a hindrance than a help to getting what we want in life. At least when we were high, we didn't feel so bad about ourselves; we could escape these terrible feelings of failure, of being let down by life. Doubts assail us about why we've chosen to get sober; we may resist the self-labeling of alcoholic or drug addict. This unease is not limited to beginners: decades down the line, you may—in fact, probably will—suffer various crises of faith that might be summed up by the title of an old Peggy Lee song: "Is That All There Is?"

The definition of *successful sobriety* central to this book not only includes staying away from drugs and alcohol once you've determined they're killing you, it also includes feeling *satisfied* with your sober life. *Satisfaction* is, however, a slippery idea. While my experience and the experience of recovering addicts with whom I've talked convince me that the rewards of a sober, conscious life are wondrous, unmistakable, and available to all of us, they're also often hard to quantify. One hard lesson all of my recovering friends have taught me is that

the whole structure of our old reward systems has to be
rethought. The very way we imagine that the *universe*
works may have to be rethought. This fundamental re-
thinking can take you to some very strange, surprising,
and ultimately satisfying places, but generally not without requiring that you undergo a fair amount of grumpi-
ness, frustration, and sometimes even a sense of
profound loss and mourning.

As before, routes through this Pilgrim's Progress of
emotions are as varied as the people who take them. My
message of hope here is that the route *can* be taken.

Playing in the Dark: A New View of Desire

"When I heard alcohol referred to as a 'superego sol-
vent,'" Mike says, "it fit. Alcohol—with some coke
chasers, and I don't mean Coca-Cola—got rid of my
conscience. Getting rid of that monster was an inde-
scribable relief. I could *accept* myself more drunk and
high—that's the long and the short of it. I wasn't quite
the unattractive screwup I thought I was otherwise. Stuff
just didn't bother me the way it did when I wasn't high."

Mike, who describes himself as "a superannuated Peter Pan, forty-four going on about fourteen," is a short,
slight, wiry man whose most recent and greatest love in
sobriety has turned out to be running. "I was so physically wasted for decades—I've been sober about six
years, and I started drinking hard and doing coke when I
was about thirteen—that I was rarely anything but a
physical wreck all through my so-called youth. Now that
I'm running, I feel strong and alive in a way I never did
before in my life. I was a total failure in everything be-

fore. I just barely got through high school, started at a local community college but flunked out within a couple months, and attached myself to a series of extremely abusive lovers who fed me, sometimes hit me, but most important made it possible for me to keep drinking and doing drugs."

Mike, who is gay, says that it's only been in the past few years that he's acknowledged his sexuality at all fully to himself, which

In my case, means acknowledging that I still hate myself. Good old internalized homophobia. My parents hit the roof when they discovered gay pornography in my clothes hamper—I was thirteen. They threatened to send me to a military boys school, which they maintained would "make a man out of me." Now I wish they had. Military strictness would have been preferable to the constant yelling and kicks in the ass I kept getting at home. I appeased them by agreeing to go to some aversion-therapy expert, who put me through a series of really horrible experiments, none of which changed my sexuality one whit, but all of which made my trust of anyone, which was already plummeting to zero, disappear entirely. Actually, that's not entirely true. I have a younger sister who was about ten years old when my parents first whaled into me for being gay. She didn't know what was going on, but she stuck by me. She's the only person I've known who gave me anything like unconditional love. But it felt like too little; the rest of the world seemed to be on a rampage against me. The rest of the world didn't seem to want any part of me. So I got high. A lot. I was young, skinny, and I guess attractive. I mean, teenagers don't realize what a fleeting prize their youth is. A series of, shall we say, "older" men took me on, beat me up, kept me high, eventually threw me out. I slept around a lot; it's a miracle I don't have AIDS, but somehow I was spared that. I often wonder why. But while AIDS wasn't killing me, drugs and alcohol were. I ended up in the hospital numerous times, the last time with a sick kidney, liver, and severe anemia. The last lover I had was a heroin addict who overdosed when I was in the hospital. I was too numb to care very much. All I knew was that I had no home to go home to; when he died, his apartment died with him.

Mike was thirty-seven by this time and had no idea where to go. His sister, Claire, came to his rescue. "Claire had tried to keep in touch with me all through the years, but I was so out of it most of the time and so basically ashamed of the mess my life was that I rarely returned her calls, lying to her that everything was okay when I did. I guess I still thought of her as my 'good little sister,' and I didn't want her to see the sordid creature her older brother had become. But somehow, the last time, she found out I was in the hospital and that I had no place to go. She and her boyfriend took me in. And it's really because of them that I got sober."

Mike did not go to AA, although Claire had lots of what she called "program friends" who were more than willing to take Mike to meetings. Claire's boyfriend had been to AA as well and swore by the Twelve Steps. But Mike said, "I just didn't like the idea of spilling my guts out in front of a huge group of people. I knew that wasn't going to be the way for me. It was hard—I don't know where I got the nerve to stand up to all those well-meaning people. And I felt guilty about it, like I was letting them down because I just wouldn't 'get it.' " But Claire's love, common sense, and care-giving Mike meals, a clean place to sleep, someone to talk to, some-one who didn't require anything of him in those first fragile months of being off drugs and alcohol—were, Mike now believes, "what really got me through. I knew I didn't want to waste myself anymore with drugs and booze. I think my last lover's death marked the end of that for me. I'd just had enough. But I also didn't feel like a born-again saint or that some spiritual awakening hap-pened to me. I just felt relieved. More 'normal,' I sup-pose. Even maybe that I was *human*. I hadn't felt human before—I'd always felt like some kind of scurrying little rat."

Mike got a job at a local department store and sur-prised himself by a series of quick promotions. "I seemed to have a talent I never knew I had for dealing with vendors and psyching out the market, predicting what would sell. I became an assistant buyer and starting dealing with representatives of several major clothes de-signers. I amazed myself by discovering I was *good* at something: this had never happened before!" Mike's work brought him into contact with a lot of other gay men who worked in the fashion industry. "Once, this guy asked me out to dinner, and I knew it wasn't for business. I freaked," Mike says. "My only experience of dating—well, I'd never had any. Basically sex to me meant getting drugged up and allowing yourself to be raped."

Mike was too afraid to pursue anything with this first man, but the experience brought the idea of sex back into his mind with a vengeance, and he started missing some of the old let-'er-rip times he'd had.

I'd started going to therapy by this time—that was one suggestion Claire made that I did take—and I liked my therapist. I felt from the start that I could talk to him, even about the sexual stuff that had started up again, started to kick my ass. As I began to explore my sexual past, my fantasies, this huge dark part of me I thought I'd left behind with alcohol and drugs overwhelmed me again—first slowly, seeping up, then explosively, like a volcano. My therapist told me to hang on—it was just my libidinal self crying out for expression after years of being repressed, he said—but I thought of it as a big evil spirit, something so much more powerful than I that when it welled up in me I turned into its complete slave. It was about this time I started running. I thought maybe physically I could just *drive* this sex thing into another channel, exhaust myself by running harder and faster and longer every time I went out. But it worked in reverse. It made me *more* aware of my body, not less. I loved the feeling of pushing myself, of sweating, of being a physical being. At the end of a run, far from driving sex out of my mind, it was all I wanted to do. I was desperate to make contact.

But the contact I wanted to make was the *old* contact. However much healthier I'd become by running, by being sober, by taking care of myself physically, I had no desire to meet some "white bread" nice guy. Rediscovering myself physically made me crave the old abusive sex, which was, after all, the only sex I'd ever known. I started responding to SM ads in gay papers, phone ads, especially the ones from—you guessed it—self-described "abusive older" guys. It seemed the cruelest turn of fate that my fantasies centered on, fed from, the very violence I'd suffered as a child and in old those drugged relationships. I felt sick in every way: nauseous, mentally ill, emotionally crippled—I couldn't escape this great black demon of my sexual fantasies now that I'd found it. My therapist kept telling me it was okay, to hang on, it was a normal part of me. But it didn't feel anything like a normal part of me.

Feeling driven, Mike began to meet some of the men he contacted through ads.

The really awful part was, now that I wasn't drugging or drinking, I couldn't respond physically. Sure, I could run—my body was in better condition—but, well, I was impotent. When I thought about it, I realize that's how I was a lot when I was high all the time, but then it didn't bother me as much. In fact, being wasted was a good excuse I used a lot. Now it just seemed like another dismal failure for which I had no excuse. The fact that I couldn't respond sexually with my body—even though I craved contact with my imagination, my fantasies, my mind— just made the split inside of me more obvious and painful. Since I couldn't bring myself any real genital pleasure, my entire focus with the guys I was with was on satisfying *them*. So I'd put myself through elaborate scenarios I often discovered I didn't want to complete, but I wouldn't leave until the other man got what he wanted. It's like my sexual fantasies were mocking me! Enticing me into situations I hated once I was actually in them. I began to think that the only way to deal with this horrible split in me was to start taking drugs, start drinking again. At least then the pain wouldn't be so bad. At least then I'd have some way of blocking out my self-hatred and feeling of inadequacy. I started to have really way-out, self-flagellating sadomasochistic fantasies, where I'd be beaten into unconsciousness—it was like I was trying to kill off some part of myself. Claire, my therapist, the "reasonable" people I knew at work who thought I was so talented and good at my job—none of them knew what I was really like. I couldn't let them know, either. If they had an inkling what was really going on inside me, they'd flee me in horror.

Mike takes a deep breath.

Then it hit me—well, *hit* is too strong a word—it quietly, for the first time, *occurred* to me that I had never allowed myself to even *think* about sex, sober, before this. Of course it was beating my ass in sobriety! It was so powerful and alien to me. I had always responded, from early puberty on, to sexual urges by getting high, so that I wouldn't really have to face them, wouldn't really in some sense have to *feel* them as completely as I was now feeling them sober. I brought this idea in to my therapist, and he beamed. He welcomed me as a kind of newcomer—which he said we pretty much all are, all the time, because we're always facing a moment we've never faced before. And sometimes this is going to be frightening, especially when the moment we're facing is sexual, tied to our fiercest, most primal feelings and urges.

It was a simple idea on the face of it, but it's turned into a profound revelation: I accepted that *I didn't know how to deal with sex sober.* What this seemed to make possible was the idea that I could *learn* more about what sex meant to me sober. That's really all I had discovered. And while the demons are still sometimes frightening, this acceptance that I don't have to be sexually perfect or in any other way perfect is slowly taking root. Strangely, my ability to be around people in general is benefiting from this new letting up on myself, this permission I'm giving myself to *not know* everything. I'm a little more at ease. Not really with sex yet, but with people, people at work, my sister, friends. I'm not quite so afraid anymore. I don't hate myself as much anymore.

As Mike has learned that he can tolerate his own desires more completely, he has also learned—and relearned ("it takes continual reminding," he says)—that there's always more help to be had, help that can be tailored precisely to whatever problems or obstacles come up. "I've suffered from chronic depression my whole life, which I know is linked to why I drank and drugged so much, but which I've only begun to understand better now that I'm sober. After talking for months about it with my therapist, he suggested that I go to a psychiatrist colleague of his from whom I could get a prescription for an antidepressant, Zoloft. At first I was afraid—I mean, I don't want to take aspirin, much less any other kind of drug—but I guess I accept that I'm a chemical being as well as a spiritual, mental, and physical one, and some part of this depression is biochemical. Anyway, the Zoloft has helped. An edge has been taken off. It works for me."

Mike also says that his goal is not to rid himself of his sexual fantasies—or any other feelings or thoughts that come up, however threatening they at first appear to be.

My goal is to look at them and decide, maybe, if I can learn from them, play with them, have some power over them, maybe even have some fun with them. Sometimes this means acting out a fantasy; sometimes it means, at least down the line, laughing at it. It often means making mistakes, sometimes not feeling so great about certain decisions I've made but still learning from them. One amazing discovery is that I can *leave* a situation if it's bad for me. I don't have to wait out every encounter, sexual or otherwise, to the bitter end. I can pay attention to my own desires and discomfort.

I guess the main idea I'm gaining from the help I'm

getting is that I've got more *choice* than I thought I had. The world isn't split up into neat good-and-bad, *X*-always-equals-*Y*, either/or propositions. I once thought that getting blasted out of my mind was the only way I could have sex or deal with it in any way. I realize now I was throwing grenades at myself, trying to explode huge aspects of my sexuality so that I wouldn't have to *see* them. Now I want to see them. Now it seems like an adventure I can undertake without it killing me.

More Than the Sum of Your Parts

That life might be an adventure you can undertake without it killing you is a fascinating idea to thirty-four-year-old Jeanne, an art dealer in New York. Born in Paris, Jeanne asks, "Can you imagine a French person not drinking wine? It's unthinkable. It certainly was unthinkable to me. Sometimes I thank God I'm in New York and not in Paris; drinking Perrier with your dinner is acceptable here in a way that I can't imagine it ever being in France. You may think this is superficial. It is not. Giving up wine meant giving up a huge symbolic part of myself. I no longer define myself the way I did. It is frightening when you change something so fundamental as your basic idea of who you are."

Jeanne was only able to accept that her drinking had become uncontrollable five years into her New York life.

I was not only French in France, I was Jewish, which meant that being an alcoholic was, to my family and friends, a double impossibility. French *and* Jewish? I was thought genetically *impossible* to be alcoholic. And so any excess on my part—and as I went through my twenties, my excesses became quite remarkable—were regarded as simple human weakness, a reason for feeling shame. The concept of alcoholism as an illness over which you had no control was completely foreign. Any attempt to see excess drinking as anything more than bad behavior was ridiculed. My father would laugh at the Americans and all of their psychologizing. We felt very superior to all of those Californians who went on silly excursions to "find themselves," and certainly we looked down on anyone who admitted in public that they were drunks or drug addicts, as if this were a reason for praise. Americans seemed like little puppy dogs, yapping out whatever was in their minds, jumping all over each other with childish indiscretion. In fact, that was my father's favorite muttered malediction: *indiscrète*.

Of course, I now realize that my father had a very bad drinking problem, which he was under great stress to hide and ignore, and that alcoholism is far more rampant in France than any Frenchman wants to admit. As a child I grew up drinking wine; as an adult I slowly realized I couldn't live without a greater and greater daily dose of alcohol. But culturally, I could not admit it. So this pain of feeling sick and abnormal, always making excuses for why I had acted so badly the night before, was something I felt doomed to keep secret. When my Paris gallery transferred me to New York, I was thrilled. I felt I could invent a new Jeanne there—nobody would know about the sickness I felt inside me—I would get over this "weakness," this *maladie,* simply by getting over the Atlantic Ocean. I would leave it and everything bad about me behind.

However, Jeanne found she was just as alcoholic in New York as she had been in Paris.

At first the exoticism of being French got me through some of the embarrassing situations I'd get into: flirting inappropriately with clients and artists, passing out at parties, then losing my temper the next day at meetings because I had such bad hangovers. I think most people thought this was all somehow because I was a temperamental European. But I was sick and getting sicker. Because of me, our international gallery was beginning to lose clients. Word got out that I was "trouble." I work on a commission basis, and the gallery owners encouraged buyers to do business with other people in the company. I got in terrible debt, borrowing from everyone I could think of, then spending the money without a thought, foolishly, on clothes and wine.

My life was spiraling down at an alarming rate. Finally, at a party where I was once again getting drunk and becoming my usual obnoxious self, the host came up behind me and hissed into my ear that I was making a fool of myself and if I wanted to stay, I would have to stop drinking. I was shocked—and then more angry than I can ever remember being. I blew up right there, accused this person of inexcusable bad manners, raising my voice so that everyone at the party could hear. Then, in full self-righteous fury, I stormed out, slamming the door. How dare he say such a thing! I heard my father's bitter voice in my head. On the elevator ride down from the penthouse I'd stormed out of, I spat out every curse I'd ever heard him make about boorish Americans and how impossible it was to put up with them—luckily no one else was in the elevator! Somehow I staggered into a cab, still muttering to myself, and got myself home, where, as usual, I passed out. But the next morning, awakening with my usual deadly hangover, I didn't do something as usual: I actually *remembered* the night before; every detail of it came seeping slowly and painfully to consciousness. As I relived it all, I felt a devastating humiliation. Somehow the most painful moment was the entry of my father's voice, the curses I'd spat out that I'd learned from him—I knew had become as sick and vengeful and bitter as he was. I knew, at that moment, that I was worse than sick—I was somehow *dying*. It was as if something were being strangled in me. I panicked. I actually felt my throat constricting; I could barely breathe. Who could I call to help me? My hand shot out desperately for the phone, I dialed 911 and gasped out that I needed an ambulance.

Jeanne shakes her head and laughs quietly. "I'll never forget the looks on the faces of the medics who came to pick me up. I was a crazy person, my nightgown half on, half off me, my hair sticking out, gasping in French that I was dying. I must have looked like I'd lost my mind." She allowed them to escort her out, becoming docile as a child, as if walking to some imprisonment she knew she deserved. "I think I really had lost my mind," Jeanne said. "I continued to mutter in French about the vengeance of God as I let them bring me downstairs in a wheelchair. Somehow I had convinced myself they were taking me to an insane asylum. That really was where I wanted to go. I wanted to be locked up, drugged, taken out of this impossible life, and taken care of completely."

At first the medics believed that the raving Jeanne had overdosed on hallucinogenic drugs. But by the time she got to the hospital, one of them, picking up on signs he knew all too well because he himself was a recovering alcoholic (not least of which was the unmistakable stale smell that seeped from her pores) diagnosed her more correctly: a touch of alcoholic dementia and one hell of a hangover. "It was because of this man that I was put into the hospital's—what do the patients call it?—drunk tank. When I realized where I was, I threw an incredible tantrum. How dare they call me a drunk! Did they not know who I was? An important French art dealer? How could such a person be a drunk? The admitting counselor, a harried but gentle, middle-aged, maternal woman, let me rave for a while and then told me that I could leave if I wanted to, but that I might benefit from staying. I nearly turned my back on her, then I thought, what am I going back to? My throat began to constrict again. I turned back toward her. 'Do with me what you will,' I said nobly as if I were Joan of Arc. And I stayed for four weeks of rehabilitation."

What Jeanne began to face in these four weeks and in the year and a half since those four weeks was on one level simple: she had long been completely, physically, and emotionally addicted to alcohol. "It's hard enough for the average American to accept something like this, but for me it was more than a stigma. It was as if I had never known what I was. It was as if I were some alien being, and now this fact was revealed to me!" Jeanne was subjected to mandatory AA meetings in the rehab. Although they baffled her at first—"I couldn't get used to people admitting to such horrible behavior in public!"—she did begin to hear that everyone felt, in some way, as "alien" to themselves as she felt to herself.

In the days, weeks, and months after her departure from the rehab, Jeanne has managed to hook up with some women's AA meetings that, she says, "have given me the first few true friends I've ever had. But they've also gotten me to question some basic ideas in a way that doesn't threaten me. Recently I joined a women's group that departs from AA, that sees AA as limited because it does not adequately address the needs of women. Somehow, as I've questioned my father's voice in me, I've begun to wonder who I might be *without* that voice. I have never been attracted to politics, and I do not see myself as any kind of feminist activist, but I also realize I have never really looked into who I am—as a woman, as a human being, as what I now accept is a recovering alcoholic. I always thought of myself before as a collection of inescapable traits: French, my father's daughter, Jewish, artistic. Now, slowly, with the help of two or three close women friends, I am starting to believe that there might be a larger, deeper, and less categorizable self growing— I am more than the sum of those very limited parts."

Jeanne is clear about what has kept her sober these past months: "support from these friends, especially the women I've met in this 'splinter' AA group I'm now going to." Her work life has changed considerably.

My gallery knew I was in the hospital, and they had discovered by calling me there what division of the hospital I was in. When I got back to work, most people were actually relieved to see me. They had known that my problems were more a matter of alcohol than of French temperament, and they were very supportive. What amazed me is not only that my compulsion to drink had, thank God, lifted from me, but that I could still be interesting. I didn't need the boost of alcohol to unleash my opinions, my individuality. I was afraid at the beginning that not drinking would mean that I simply wouldn't be able to talk to anyone anymore. But I *could* talk to people. In fact, I could talk more clearly. I was less apt to lose my temper, although my work in my women's group tells me that I still have as yet unfathomed anger to deal with, much of it bound up in my feelings about my father. But I had not lost my *mystery*. I am just as interesting as I ever was. My sense of art, my ability to understand it, the talent I have always had for conveying the beauty of a painting to someone else—prospective buyers not least among them!—have if anything *increased*, widened, become richer and more reliable. It's as if I am rediscovering what was there all the time but that I didn't trust could be there without alcohol opening the door. This self that has unique talents and a point of view and a center of gravity needs no external lubrication to get going. I have just begun to realize this, but I am heartened by what I continue to find: more of *me*, more of someone who finds that she *can* exist in the world without fleeing from it or hiding behind various identifying traits. I am more, much more, than a thirty-four-year-old French, Jewish, alcoholic, artistic female.

"I Didn't Get Sober to Be a Saint": Machismo and Sobriety

Prejudices about what a "man," a "woman," an "American," an "alcoholic," or an "addict" are supposed to be almost always bite the dust in sobriety. When we start to live consciously, the world simply isn't categorizable in the ways it used to be when we drank or drugged. This has been a wild, roller-coaster ride of a revelation to Jorge, a twenty-eight-year-old Puerto-Rican-born carpenter, former boxer, and ex-husband with two kids whose violent drug- and alcohol-induced blackouts not only ruined his marriage but put him into jail.

"Don't give me any of that AA shit," Jorge warns me when he hears that I'm working on a book about sobriety. "I've had it up to here with that crap. All that higher power, holding hands, and praying to God stuff—and all that whining. I had enough of that after the second meeting I went to. Sure I had to sit through more than two meetings when I was locked up, but man, my mind wandered, and I *let* it wander. I'd already decided that booze and drugs had kicked my ass and that I didn't want to do that to myself any more. I didn't have to go on whining about it for the rest of my life."

Jorge does, however, make it clear that his life is very different postjail and post–booze and drugs: "I don't hang with the same guys I used to. They're just fucking themselves up, man. Standing around on the street, getting high, acting tough, feeling like they're hot shit. Man, they ain't nothing. I got better things to do than hang with those losers. My wife won't take me back—I don't blame her, after the shit I put her through—but she sees I've changed. She lets me see my two little girls every weekend. I bring them toys—I love those kids, man. And they love me, too. It's like they have a father now; they didn't have one before. And I'm making money now. I'm a hell of a carpenter. I never knew I had this talent until I started doing woodworking in jail. I can make you a whole damned library, like in a mansion. The best wood, best finishes, perfect corners, perfectly fitted moldings. I won't leave a job until it's done right. I'm a friggin' artist."

However, Jorge quickly assures me that he hasn't turned into a saint just because he no longer drinks and drugs. "Let all those damned Twelve-Step people be saints if they want to. I'm gonna have a good time." Having a good time, though, has proven a little more elusive now that he no longer gets high. "There are times, you know, I need a woman, so I just go out and get one. I don't mean 'date.' Hell, why you wanna go out with some lady you don't know, spend a lot of money on dinner, talk to her, maybe get a kiss, meet her the next week for another dinner you pay for, maybe you get a kiss and a hug, then finally, four, five, six weeks later, you're out a lot of money, but you finally get into bed, and the chick thinks you're gonna marry her, plus the sex is lousy? Then she starts calling you all the time, saying that you're a no-good bum, that you have no feelings, that you're a damned ape, that you said you loved her but now you won't marry her—" Jorge snorts. "Who needs that shit? When I get horny, man, I buy me a woman for the night. She does what I pay her to do, that's the end of it. Or I'll go to one of those strip joints, you know, where the women get naked right over you, make you nuts, then you meet them a little later, and . . . Man, what's wrong with that? Takes care of business just fine."

Except it doesn't, Jorge finally admits, always "take care of business."

Okay, it's not like that's a great life or anything. I guess I don't always feel so great after it's over. So much was wrapped up in getting high—I mean, to go with a whore, you gotta feel like you're *partying*—at least I do. And now, you know, I just plain notice more. I see the lady better. I see the lines on her face. I see when she seems a little frightened or just plain out of it. I can't ignore her so completely any more. It's like she's not just some sex toy. And I hate that. I'll be honest with you, if I could just turn these ladies back into sex toys, I'd be a lot happier.

But the last lady I went with, I can't fucking believe it,

but we ended up *talking* for a half hour. Then we didn't even *do* it. Man, what the hell was I doing, paying money to talk to some lady? Was I crazy? I was pissed at myself. Turning into a friggin' wuss. But this lady didn't seem happy. And she said—hell, at first I thought it was a line—she said, "You're different from other men." Yeah, that's what they all say, right? Except I could tell she meant it. And I realized then that the only men she saw were basically bombed out of their minds. She told me she was a lesbian. Man, a *lesbian!* I was fascinated. Why was she going with guys? She said she just looked at it like a job, did it as well as she could, and that was it. Why was she telling me all this stuff? I don't know. She said I made her feel more comfortable, like she didn't have to lie about anything. Tell you the truth, I didn't want to have sex with her after all. I mean, hell, she'd be thinking of some other woman, not me! But it was more than that. I'd actually seen her as a person. Damn, I hate when that happens. But lately it seems to be happening more and more.

I wouldn't mind getting involved with a lady again, settle down, have someone, you know, to go home to. But I don't know if I can do that ever again. It's like, I always had some escape before, when stuff got too bad. I guess I do miss getting high, getting blasted. I've been hitting the gym again a couple nights a week. I used to box, did it professionally for a couple years when I was a kid, maybe nineteen, twenty. Problem was I hated the discipline. I wanted to get high. I loved beating guys up, and the trainer said I got good instincts. But all that roadwork and working out every day is a drag. Basically I got thrown out of the place because I kept on coming in high. But now that I'm clean I'm going back, hitting the heavy bag, doing some sparring. It helps a little. It helps to *hit* something. There's like some, I don't know, *force* inside me that's gotta get out somehow. I guess I always let it out before when I got high and wild. And some of it goes into my being a perfectionist with my woodworking. But sometimes, you know, you just gotta *slam* something.

Jorge's world of people is centered almost entirely on the guys with whom he works for a contracting company. "The guys at work are cool about my not drinking. Before they used to have beers on breaks, now we're all drinking Snapple ice tea. They're good guys. From all the hell over the place, too: Greece, Pakistan, Nigeria. There's this whole world of hardworking immigrants I never knew about who save every penny and send it home to their wives and kids. It's opened my eyes. There's a lot more different people on this planet than I knew about before."

Jorge says he feels for the first time

I got a life. But it's like, I don't know, *disturbing* in a way it never was before. I mean, before, stuff was real simple. Basically, you got high. And then you let yourself do whatever the fuck you wanted to do. Now it's not like that anymore. I don't know exactly what direction I'm heading, except I'd like to get enough business to work independently some day, so that I don't have to go where some contractor tells me to go. I don't know what the hell I'm gonna do about a woman. I don't know even what I *want* right now. I'm sure as hell not gonna keep myself from having a good time, I know that. But part of having a good time is playing with my kids. I guess there are more options than I thought there were. Sometimes I feel like a kid myself—I can't wait for the weekend to come when I can play with my little girls. Last week I got them a puppy. You should've seen them. They were jumping up and down, they were so happy. I've never *seen* any two kids so happy. It was amazing. I'd actually done something that made them that way. It's strange to feel like you're, you know, *loved*. It's a little scary. I'm not sure I always like it. It's like when somebody loves you, you feel this responsibility to be there for them, not to let them down. Sometimes I think anyone who'd love me would have to be a jerk. But then I look at my little girls. They don't seem to mind that I'm a jerk—or that I was one. They seem to love me anyway.

Jumping Off the Life Raft

The worlds that are opening up for Mike, Jeanne, and Jorge are opening up slowly and unpredictably. It's hard not to be baffled by the new rules and the new assumptions that conscious life seems to encourage us to consider, take on, and internalize. As Jorge put it, it was simple before: "basically you got high," then you did whatever you wanted to do. Now, basically, we *don't* get high, and it's not always clear what we want to do. The old rewards don't always seem as enticing.

When I stopped drinking, I didn't stop going to bars. In fact, for a few months I'd spend every day after work in the same piano bar I went to when I drank, this time nursing seltzer with lime, but otherwise trying to respond to the environment the way I used to respond to it. I'd bring a stack of magazines—the celebrity pulp kind—and try to interest myself in what Elizabeth Taylor or Michael Jackson was doing. I'd try to talk to my old friends, but they no longer seemed like a slightly more bohemian cast of *Cheers*. Unlike the cast of *Cheers,* all of my friends just got drunk and, frankly, less funny and more boring. But I was struck by something else, something more disturbing. People seemed to be clinging— sometimes literally—to the bar. It was like a life raft. And I realized that this bar had been a life raft for me, too. I wasn't there, as I thought for so long I had been, for "fun." I was there because I couldn't imagine where else to be. And that was the most stifling feeling to me: my "friends" were in this bar, it seemed to me at this moment, because in some sense they felt they had no choice. They *had* to be there. And I flashed back on all the times when I wouldn't pay rent so that I could spend money and nights in this bar; I flashed to the stormy afternoons I'd rush to the bank (before the days of ATMs) so that I'd have enough money to spend in this bar. In other words, this bar ruled me as if I were a bee and it were the hive and the queen was a bottle of vodka.

During these vestigial months at the bar, I had a few subsidiary revelations, too: for one, I discovered that I didn't *like* reading celebrity pulp magazines. Strange, I always thought I had! But, sober, I realized that reading trash had always accompanied drinking vodka. It was a way I could allow my mind to check out while the vodka was doing its best to help me do the same thing chemically. But now, on some obvious and fundamental level, I simply wasn't "checking out" anymore. More than that, I discovered that I didn't *want* to check out. I wanted to *see* what was around me. And what I saw in this bar was a hive of very frightened and very driven "bees." Some metamorphosis had happened to me without my especially wanting it: all I knew eventually was that I wanted to see what life was like outside the door, away from this place. I wanted to jump off the life raft and see if I could swim.

Recently, more than nine years after taking that plunge, I got a call from someone I knew from my "hive" days, someone with whom I drank, someone who, sheerly from his regular presence and a sort of cynical mordant wit, had become a "friend." Like every one of my other bar friends, however, when I stopped drinking, he and I discovered that we stopped having anything to talk about. I don't know that I'll ever exactly understand the mysterious absence that giving up alcohol creates. It's as if something essential, something you needed to define yourself, something that connects you automatically to other drinkers, has been utterly erased. The main "language" you spoke is suddenly gone. There were so many awkward silences in that bar between Joe and me when I stopped drinking. So, after all these years, I was curious to see if that "erasure" still existed.

Joe actually was more of a coke head than a drunk. He *loved* cocaine; he was always running to the men's room for another line. Back in the early eighties, Joe parlayed his aggressive quick wit into a series of flashy advertising jobs, which put him in flashy settings—mansions in northern California, penthouse apartments on Park Avenue—all owned by other people but which were offered to him as perks of the jobs he'd managed to talk his way into. I'd never understood how he was able to pull off these coups until he let out one evening that he also performed the function of drug supplier. Joe was really getting by on cocaine earnings; the advertising work was a foil for the only thing that really counted to him: cocaine.

Now, Joe was homeless. He was wearing his belongings in a knapsack on his back. He'd managed to secure a clean shirt and pants the day he met me, but otherwise he made no secret of the mess his life had become. He was trying to negotiate the welfare system of New York, primarily to get him a doctor who would prescribe anti-depressants as well as to give him some kind of money to "live on" (buy drugs). He had been thrown out by every friend, every lover, every member of his family. Sleeping on park benches, Joe begged for money and, because he still more or less had his looks, was now thinking of becoming a prostitute, hoping to sell himself in parks to furtive men. Joe was not gay, but it seemed an easy way to make money, hiding in a bush, dropping your pants, closing your eyes, and allowing some disembodied mouth to do the rest for a fee of—what would I suggest he charge? Since I am gay, he thought I might have some advice for him about how to pursue this line of work. I told him what little I knew, gave him a lunch at a nearby diner, then awaited the real question he'd come to ask: could I lend him some money? He could see the tension in my face. I didn't like the feeling of being used. Then he said something more heartbreaking than he knew: "At least you agreed to see me. Nobody else will." It wasn't a sob story—it was the truth. He'd "borrowed," lied, stolen, connived, his way out of the lives of anyone he'd ever known. He was steeling himself now for one more inevitable kick in the butt.

I gave him five dollars and wished him well. I left him at the booth of the diner, sipping a cup of coffee, eying the two-dollar tip I'd left the waiter. I doubt the waiter got his tip.

When I left Joe in that diner, I left a ghost of myself. I left a variation on a theme of what might have become of me—had I not stopped drinking (and had I lived). But the experience brought into sharp relief exactly what my departure from drinking had gained me: I'd escaped from the hive, the prison, a supposed "life raft" that had really been drifting toward death. Joe was a driven "bee" who hadn't realized there wasn't any more honey in the hive he kept buzzing around. He didn't know there were other hives. He had no idea there was anywhere else to go, anything else to do but what he'd always done. Through some inexplicable experience of grace, I *had* learned that there were other things to do, places to go.

Mike, Jeanne, and Jorge have let us know that there are other hives; there are many more places to explore than the ones we knew when we got high. However, they're often unnervingly unfamiliar. Success, pleasure, satisfaction, "having a good time," are not the black-and-white business we imagined them to be. There are more subtle currents at work. There are more ways to think about ourselves, to decide who we *are*, than we once knew. As Mike said, "I guess the main idea I'm gaining from the help I'm getting is that I've got more *choice* than I thought I had. The world isn't split up into neat good-and-bad, X-always-equals-Y, either/or propositions." As Jeanne stated, "It's as if I am rediscovering what was there all the time but that I didn't trust could be there without alcohol opening the door. This self that has unique talents and a point of view and a center of gravity needs no external lubrication to get going." And as Jorge said most simply, "I got a life."

At the very least, we learn this: having a life turns out to be a much more interesting proposition when we're sober than it ever was when we weren't.

Chapter Four

Loneliness

Recently, hungry and craving grease, I went out to a local Nathan's fast-food restaurant for a quick lunch. I sat down with my hot dog and fries a table away from two people, who at first peripheral glance seemed to me to be an elderly woman and a tiny child. A more direct glance told me that the "tiny child" was in fact also an elderly woman who was evidently suffering from some degenerative bone and muscle disease, a disease I had to believe, judging from the completeness with which her body had sunk into itself, had been lifelong. She was complaining about a long list of other fast-food restaurants—pizza, egg roll, and hamburger counters—at which she had been badly treated. "I should have walked out," the tiny woman said, "when that man gave me my pizza and it was too hot. I told him I only wanted it warm. I had paid for it already, but I still should have walked out. Then he would have realized what he'd done."

The larger woman was not sympathetic. "But where *was* the pizza place?" she replied impatiently. "You said it was near the Chinese place, and there's no pizza place near the Chinese place!" My fantasy that the larger woman was the deformed woman's friend couldn't hold up. The larger woman seemed annoyed by everything the tiny woman said.

I tried to imagine the tiny woman in any situation where she would not be overlooked, shunned, or pitied. I tried to imagine dressing her up and putting her in a cocktail party, watching and listening to the laughter and attempted seductions among the "normal" people around her. Had this woman ever had a romance? Had she ever had sex? Had she ever had any secret, shameful moment of completion? Had she ever felt for even one moment in public that she wasn't a freak? All of the daily activities I took for granted—going to the post office, buying a quart of milk at the corner, meeting someone for lunch, planning to see my lover on the weekend—all of these human interactions seemed to me suddenly miraculous. This woman would not seem "normal" in any of these situations. Her physical disfigurement had to seem to her a curse she could never shed, never for a moment forget.

Why was I so upset? Why couldn't I finish my lunch? Why did I have to leave? Why could I not bear even one more moment listening to this unfriendly conversation between these two women?

My lunch experience stayed with me for hours, into the night and the next day, and finally crystallized into the realization that *I* felt, had felt in the past and some-times still felt, as emotionally disfigured as the tiny woman at Nathan's was physically disfigured. Some Dorian Gray dynamic was going on: she looked how I felt. And I found it so painful to look at her, to listen to her, because she had displayed her pain so blatantly, so overtly. Like so many other alcoholics and addicts, I had striven my whole life to hide my pain, to pretend I knew what I was doing, to make out as if I were "normal." Inside, sometimes, even in sobriety, I still felt horribly abnormal. And here this woman was, *flaunting* her pain out in the open. Rationally I knew this was a terribly narcissistic, self-serving way of looking at her—who knew that she didn't have a wonderful life, many friends, a loving family, a great feeling of purpose in the world? At any rate, she may not have been as badly off as I imagined her. But my vision of her reacquainted me with how desperately badly off I used to feel, sometimes still felt, myself.

I present my Nathan's lunch story in the effort to make it clear that the loneliness so many of us feel is far more than a matter of, say, not finding the right mate. Our loneliness stems from some ancient source in each of us, a sense in which we felt, and maybe still feel, lacking, deformed, inadequate. Our loneliness is not only a cry from the soul for "contact," it is also the product of a strange, deep, reflexive shame about our own inadequate selves—an inadequacy we also often feel is somehow our fault. By a stroke of evil fate or our own stupid mismanagement of our lives, we are doomed to a kind of terminal uniqueness. We are not loved because we are not lovable. That, we believe, is the hard, frightening truth.

Does this seem too strong? Certainly many recovering men and women I know would say, "Hey, I don't feel *that* bad about myself!" But go back vividly enough to the days, hours, moments, you drank or took drugs, and you will find, I can virtually guarantee, the emotional equivalent of my tiny, deformed woman at Nathan's. And that lost soul is not automatically made to feel "found" just because you've stopped killing yourself with booze or drugs.

Surviving in the Dark

Inescapably, addiction is a disease of isolation, of acute loneliness. Every addict and alcoholic I've ever met, in or out of whatever form of recovery, has admitted to me that they feel or have felt, in some sense, unalterably separate and apart. "No matter how connected I am to other people, even in the middle of an AA meeting," a recovering friend of mine once told me, "there's always some part of me that feels isolated—like I can't really be known by anyone else."

Judging from the intense despair this loneness and loneliness can engender in us, the roots of this feeling of separateness go deep. In fact, Freud maintained that compulsive personalities (including the addict and alcoholic) find their roots in one of childhood's earliest stages: the oral stage—the infant pre-Oedipal, prelanguage stage when pleasure as well as nourishment (which means *life*) are primarily received through the mouth. Because of some profound frustration experienced at this stage, either due to a surplus or a surfeit of oral stimulation (e.g., too much or too little breast or bottle), Freud believed that compulsive personalities have a hard time feeling cared for or connected. This fuels a compulsive urge to fill themselves with something (substance or behavior) that will compensate for the emptiness they feel, assuage the longing for contact. Compulsive people want to *fill themselves up,* get more of everything, in the fear that if they don't, it will run out, and they'll be left destitute.

We don't need to turn to Freud for proof that, as alcoholics and addicts, in some deep sense we don't feel "cared for." We need only look at our own individual experience. Whatever the source of the profound disconnection so many of us feel and have felt (before, during, and after drinking and drugging), few of us haven't felt disconnected. And for a good reason. In a sense, it *is* true that we're separate and apart.

Certainly we are *connected* to each other in crucial ways. As we've seen again and again in this book, and as I expect your own experience makes clear, one of the bedrock conditions of sobriety is what we identified at the beginning: "breaking through isolation, realizing you're not alone." We can't recover, it seems, without exploring, celebrating, making rich use of what connects us: we need each other. But we also *are* alone. We enter and leave this life alone. In some ultimate way, we are unknowable by anyone else. As much as we may want to merge in a perfect union with the perfect mate (reflecting the perfect merging of us and alcohol and/or drugs or the perfect merging with Mother we longed for as infants), we inevitably end up realizing that we're separate: you're you, and I'm me, and never the twain shall *completely* meet.

Coming to terms with this inescapable loneness is a challenge to any human being seeking self-knowledge, but it seems to be especially difficult for alcoholics and addicts. As we've seen and will continue to see in this book, addictions often open a kind of window through which we are forced—in recovery anyway—to look upon the human condition with more depth and breadth than nonaddicts ever *need* to do. Alcoholics and addicts *must* examine their pain in order to heal; this seems inescapably true as I reflect on the hundreds of recovering men and women who've told me about their lives. Facing pain, nobody has to tell you, isn't a lot of fun. And a part of the pain we face in this human condition is the realization of our essential loneness. It's a small, imperceptible step from this acknowledgment of loneness to the crippling senses of loneliness and isolation that dog many of us. But, as with so much else in recovery, we can enter this dark, cold territory without destroying ourselves; we can approach it with curiosity and care, knowing that there is more to be found in this "dark" than we realized. What we find does not have to cripple us. In fact, what we find can lead us to deeper healing and serenity than we've ever known before.

The Unnerving Experience of Love

Ron, now in his early fifties, has always described himself as a loner. "Actually," he says, "*loner* still sounds human. I was something far more than a loner. I thought of myself as some entirely different species." Ron has always been a voracious reader and absorbed volumes of psychology and philosophy throughout his childhood, teenage, college, and adult years, all, he says, "in an effort to find some kind of explanation for why the hell I was on this earth. Psychology taught me that it was no wonder I felt so alienated from everyone else. My parents were completely unsuited to the task of parenting anyone. Both were chronically depressed and self-absorbed, and they each came from parents who were just as bad at the job. Most people complain that their parents lived through them, put their own hopes and dreams onto their children, and pushed their children to succeed, vicariously seeking 'success' for themselves. At least there's some kind of positive motion in that scenario. At least, screwed up though that notion of success might be, there's some *desire* for the child to make it. With me, I was my parents' dumping ground. Nothing I did was adequate. Every negative feeling and belief about the world they had was projected onto me. I felt like some kind of character out of Thomas Hardy—you ever read *Jude the Obscure*? The kid Jude fathers is a kind of total mistake from the moment of conception, doomed from the start. That's how I've always felt—like a really bad mistake."

Ron's mother died a painful death from cancer when he was in his early twenties. His father, who Ron says drank nearly constantly after his mother's death, shot himself in the head a few years afterward. "It's tempting to whine on and on about the harm these people did to me, and sometimes I do. But the harm's there whether I whine on about it or not. What I *do* about the damage is something I feel I'm just learning about now."

Ron says he followed his father's lead in one regard: "Spiritually I've decided I really can't bump myself off. I believe in past lives and in the idea that the karma you create in this life dogs you into the next. Killing myself would just bring me back as a more miserable creature than I am in this life. But while I've made a pact with myself not to do myself in with a gun to the temple, I did mimic my father by *drinking* my head off, which, after all, is a way of killing yourself, too."

Alcohol gave Ron his first real feelings of relief. "My dad shot himself when I was about twenty-seven, which is also when I started drinking. It was so great. For the first time, this horrible feeling of not belonging, of feeling like everyone knew what the rules to this life were but me, began to, well, not disappear, but lift a little. It was like, in the world of bars, there were *other* people who felt as out of it as I did and who were finding the same medicinal help I was finding from alcohol. I didn't stop feeling like a misfit, but I realized that there were hundreds of other misfits around me who, although they didn't come from the planet *I* came from, came from planets that nobody else came from. I love the bar scenes in the movie *Star Wars* with all those different weird-looking aliens in one room. That's really the truth behind any bar full of alcoholics."

Ron had no trouble identifying himself as an alcoholic early on: "Alcoholism, after all, had a rich literary tradition—how many great writers *weren't* drunks? A drunk was something you could *be;* it was a role, something to define myself by. And, drunk, I discovered I had this wicked sense of humor, this real lashing wit. Alcohol allowed all the backed-up anger a vent, and it came out in incredible excoriations of the entire human race. I was actually, for the first time in my life, *popular* in this bar full of bohemian drunks."

In this period of popularity, Ron attracted a strong-willed woman, Ann, who decided that Ron was exactly who and what she wanted. "From the start, Ann played the conventional man's role: she seduced me, she called the shots about when and where we'd meet, she took me into her apartment, and sort of kept me as a pet. That's really what Ann wanted—someone she could own, 'fix,' direct, a kind of pet dog, I guess. That was fine with me.

I'd often fantasized about how nice it would be to get put into a padded room of some asylum and just let the 'authorities' tell me what to do. Ann became my warden, and I loved it. I stayed home, I tried my hand at writing poetry, plays, but basically I was the househusband. Yeah, we got married—a justice of the peace deal—and soon, she got herself pregnant. You know how in *The World According to Garp* Garp's mother maneuvers herself onto the only functioning part of a wounded paraplegic and gets herself pregnant? Well, that was sort of what sex was like between us. And it was great. My sexual fantasies have always been about women ravaging me—sort of taking me by force. Ann did all the work. I just kind of—*reacted.*" And, Ron says, drank. "I was on welfare then, got enough to buy some groceries and huge gallon jugs of cheap Italian white wine, which I'd nurse all day long. When Ann had our baby, little Marcie, I'd stay home, stick a bottle in Marcie's mouth, and stick a glass in mine. We were *both* nursing really. I had an incredible capacity for booze by this point. Marcie was safe—I wasn't passing out or anything. Actually, I think I was a pretty good househusband. All the booze did was keep my suicidal anger and self-hate down to a manageable level. I think of those years sometimes with longing. I knew who I was—a drunk—and what I was supposed to do—feed and diaper Marcie, and keep drinking. It was a great life for a while."

Ann, however, began to tire of it. She had an affair, Ron says, which

nearly killed me. I hadn't realized how much of my self-esteem was bound up by Ann's desire to have me as a husband—she was the first person in my life who *wanted* me. So when she had this affair with this Italian doctor—

Ann's a social worker whose clinic had medical as well as counseling offices, and this doctor was hired to run the whole place—I was devastated. It was like, on every level, Ann had found someone so far superior to me that, by contrast, I disappeared to zero. A successful, younger, handsome, wealthy *Italian*—didn't that mean he was a knockout lover? Ann made no secret of the affair. She began to sound like my parents, calling me a no-good bum. While she once thought she might make something out of me when we got married, I'd turned out to be a hopeless case—and an alcoholic, to boot. The sooner I got out of the apartment, the better. I remember getting drunker than I'd ever been, getting down on my hands and knees, begging her to keep me, not throw me out. Then I'd go into rages, throwing plates, calling her a slut. I was tormented by imagining her and this doctor making love. I saw every last sordid physical detail in my head and it made me so crazy with jealousy and hurt that it was a wonder I didn't kill her, me, and our daughter just to put an end to all of it. God knows I had fantasies of doing that. I really was a lunatic. Ann, by this time, only wanted me out of her life—and her apartment. She threatened me with police action. Finally, I gave in. I just walked out, taking not much more than a toothbrush and my last bottle of vodka—I'd changed from wine to vodka. I wasn't going drink anything *Italian* anymore!

Ron moved into a single-room-occupancy flophouse of a hotel and lived on vodka and the odd fast-food hamburger. "I hoped that this way of killing myself—gradually, with booze—would get me a better deal in the afterlife." Ron laughs to himself. "God, the screwy Rube Goldberg notions I had about God and the universe and my place in it. I spent nearly two years in a state of alcoholic dementia, reading more and more arcane stuff, Buddhist, Hindu, and Kabbalistic mysticism. I only left my room to get more vodka and junk food or to cash my welfare check. Frankly, my life had ended. I was just waiting to stop breathing."

Ron nearly got his wish. On the strength of two bottles of straight vodka consumed in one day, he went into coma. "Maybe I didn't want to die," he says, "because that day I left my door open. The superintendent of the building happened to walk down the hall, saw my door open, walked into my room to tell me I'd left it open, and found me nearly dead. He called an ambulance, and I was brought back—reluctantly—to consciousness and put in a rehab." Ron learned to like the rehab because it took care of him in the complete way he wanted to be taken care of. "Only this time, for some reason, everybody wasn't calling me a no-good drunken bum. They kept telling me I was sick and that there was something I could do about this sickness. They made me attend AA meetings, these small round-robin groups where everyone got to speak—everyone *had* to speak—and amazingly, I discovered that I liked it. I guess I liked the attention. AA meetings discourage cross-talk—nobody's supposed to talk back at you or try to persuade you of anything. It's sort of like a karaoke bar without the music or the booze: you get handed the mike, and you get to 'sing.' And, damn, I *sang*." All of the literature he'd read came out of him: "I was quoting everything from the *I Ching* to *King Lear*. I was so damned smart and funny. People started to be in awe of me a little. I liked that. I actually felt like I had some power. Like this scathing wit I was so known for in the bars was something I might be able to channel in other directions."

Ron got out of rehab, worked with an alcoholic counselor for the next two years, took a civil service exam, and placed very high, which got him a steady job in the city bureaucracy "moving paper," Ron says. In general, Ron began to have an independent life. "I was still afraid of people—I still am. But I've at least found that I don't have to be scathingly witty to get listened to. I like AA meetings because they're where I can meet people. That's how I feel about my job, too. I know I need to be around people to keep from descending back into that Heironymous Bosch hell I construct for myself when I'm alone for too long. But the loneliness, even if it doesn't often get suicidal anymore, can still sometimes take the wind out of me."

Ron labels it a miracle that he's managed to stay sober for nearly fifteen years.

I don't have regular friends, I mean, in the conventional way that people have friends they go out to movies with. I still keep pretty much to myself. But I do have people I talk to. Since they're mostly alcoholics, some of whom don't manage to stay sober, it's not exactly the most reliable bunch in the world. And the people who interest me, the people I most like to talk to, are generally the ones who are the least reliable—they're battling the same misfit feelings I battle. I know what it's like to withdraw when you feel depressed or overwhelmed, and I tend to gravitate to people who do the same thing. But while I understand this instinct to withdraw, it hurts when somebody else does the withdrawing—from me. I guess when you bring wounded people into your life, you can't expect them to stop being or acting wounded. So sometimes, like with sponsors or friends I've used as sponsors, they'll just disappear on me, and it will hurt.

My impulse is to take it much more personally than it's

ever meant; I start out being sure it's just more evidence they think I'm a no-good overneedy bum. Or I lash out at them for being no-good insensitive bums themselves. But over the years I've come to see that they're only doing what I sometimes do and that the withdrawal has more to do with their own fear and pain than with me. Eventually, what happens is that I'm able to find some forgiveness. One thing I know absolutely is that we're all on different timetables. Listening to people at AA meetings has taught me that. And I guess I'm just on a really slow one. Other people I know are moving equally slowly and not always in the same direction as I am.

Sometimes, though, other people's withdrawals, whatever the motives for them, have plunged Ron back into what can feel like inescapable blackness. "My last depression was so great," Ron says, "and my fantasies of how I'd kill myself so vivid that I actually got myself committed to a psychiatric hospital." Ron says this was the best thing he could have done for an entirely unanticipated reason. "Ever since I got sober, I kept in touch with my ex-wife, and since I've been working, I've sent her and our daughter support payments. But since my 'family' always seems just to have been visited on me—I didn't get married or have a child because I initiated anything, it was all just kind of dumped on me—I've never felt much of a connection to Marcie, our daughter. Marcie's now eighteen, a freshman in college. Sometimes, distantly—it hurt too much to really acknowledge it—I understood that I had been the absent father to her that my own father was to me. I could only guess at the damage I'd caused her. The only good parenting I'd ever done was when she was an infant and I was the househusband taking care of her. At least I went through the right motions back then. But her whole growing up was something I missed. I never *felt* like a father. And so she never really had one. But when word got to her that I was in this hospital, Marcie decided to visit me."

The meeting, Ron says, started out awkwardly.

Marcie had never sought me out before—I knew this was a big deal for her. And I had no experience being her father. I didn't know how to talk to her. I was on medication for depression, which took the edge off what might have turned into panic. It allowed me to walk to the lounge area where the nurse said she'd be. But while I know she was coming to see me because I was having a hard time, I couldn't imagine that she'd say anything *kind* to me. I mean, I'd been a total louse to her. Wouldn't she have the same burning anger toward me that I had had toward my own parents? But when I walked into the lounge and saw her—she looked beautiful, a prettier version of her mother—there was no hate in her eyes. She just seemed so completely happy to see me. I couldn't quite register this: how could she look so happy when I'd treated her so badly? She literally ran into my arms. It was terribly awkward for me. I don't really know how to hug anyone, least of all this young woman who seemed, out of nowhere, to love me. And that was it, that was what was in her eyes: love. It was completely unnerving. I had never seen love so nakedly in anyone's eyes before. It's like it burned a hole in me.

We sat down, she held my hand, asked me how I was, how I was feeling, how much longer I thought I'd be in the hospital. I felt completely tongue-tied. I searched for something witty or self-deprecating to say, and all I could do was mutter isolated words: yes, no, maybe, I guess. But even this didn't put her off. She just wanted to see me. She knew somehow how hard it had been for me. She wanted me to know that she'd *always* known something of what it was to be me.

Her own words seemed to give her courage. She took the reins, I suppose much like her mother had when I'd met her twenty years before, and the momentum of her feelings made her speak. She said that she too battled depression, that she was afraid to talk about it at home because it always made her mother launch into a tirade about "your father." She said she always felt like she had to present a perfect face to the world, that no one would accept her if she exhibited the least hint of depression, sadness. She'd always longed to talk to me because she knew that I knew what she was feeling. She'd seen me as a sensitive, hurt human being who probably knew more about the full range of feelings she had than anyone else. I interrupted in a whisper: "I'm not that smart. I don't know much at all, really." She looked into my eyes: "Yes, you do. You know what it's like to feel alone." Okay, she admitted, she also got angry at me, too; she longed to have a father who was *there*. But she also somehow understood. And whether or not she felt angry at me, she never stopped loving me. She didn't even question that. She just loved me.

She stopped talking, and we just sat on the Naugahyde couch in the harshly lit lounge for maybe five minutes, her hand covering mine. At the end of those long bewildering minutes, as my mind raced over the terribly unfamiliar territory of being loved, trying to get used to the idea that no matter what I'd done to her, my daughter actually cared about me, thought I had something to give her—anyway, at the end of those endless minutes, I did something I'd never done to her—or to anyone else—before. I put my arm around her shoulder and I gave her a kiss on the cheek. And I said, "Thank you. I love you."

Ron's discovery of love was as major a breakthrough for him, he says, as was his decision not to drink anymore.

For that moment and for a number of moments since—my daughter and I now talk to each other every week on the phone; she calls me collect from college—I had a view of myself as someone *connected* to another human being. This was completely bewildering. I realized I had so much invested in seeing myself as "apart." To *feel* another person's presence, really experience it, and to accept that this other person actually cared about me ripped to pieces the fabric of self I'd so carefully woven. No longer could I claim to be alien. Some part of me *was* connected as completely as if umbilically to somebody else. And the nature of that connection is love. Sometimes I still flee from this vision of myself as loving and lovable—hell, I often get into moods where I decide it's a all a bunch of sentimental hogwash. But then I'll hear my daughter's voice again, and I'll enter that other strange, but much more habitable universe—a universe where love has meaning.

Bringing all the other aspects of his life into this new universe is a lot of work, Ron says, that he is far from having completed. "I haven't suddenly become capable of normal friendship. I still haven't asked anyone out on a date—God knows when or if that will happen. But I do now have a clue that I *could* live in this new, connected universe if I wanted to. And I guess I do want to. Slowly, I'll move more of my baggage in. In the meantime it's enough that I visit this "love" with my daughter.

"My daughter," Ron concludes wonderingly. "I never said those words before. Now I say them all the time."

Beauty and the Beast

It's comforting to think that there's no timetable for whatever we've deemed to be progress or success, but it's an idea we rarely permit ourselves to believe to be true. No matter what road to recovery they follow, addicts and alcoholics typically look over their shoulders to see how and what everyone else is doing, generally deciding they're falling short of whatever progress they see around them. This has been the root of chronic distress for Virginia, a woman in her late forties who has been going out for the past year with a man named Greg, just past his twenty-fifth birthday.

"One of the pacts I'd made with myself when I stopped drinking five years ago," Virginia says, "is that I'd never again make myself look *ridiculous*. I can't tell you how ridiculous I made myself look when I drank. I squirm remembering some of the scenes I got into in bars, at parties, in apartments of this or that lover. Stripteases in public. Horrible fights. Sitting on my married boss's lap and massaging his—well, it wasn't his shoulders. Falling into the bed of some bar conquest or other and promptly having diarrhea on the sheets." Virginia sighs wearily. "I was an absolute mess when I drank. I lost all control. I was an embarrassment to everyone around me but especially to myself."

Becoming sober, Virginia says, has been a process of finding, accepting, and learning to live with the pieces of her personality she couldn't bear to look at before, from which she used alcohol to escape.

I am actually very shy, and drinking was the only medication I knew of that could break through my shyness. But it made the pendulum swing so far in the other direction that I turned into a lunatic. So much so that I scared myself into sobriety. You only stop doing something when *not* doing it is preferable to doing it. I turned into a monster drunk. I was sick of what alcohol did to me. So I stopped. The stuff I read about hitting bottom in recovery literature certainly applies to me. The phrase "being sick and tired of being sick and tired" is right on the money.

But I've never been to an AA meeting. I hate groups. I just can't think of myself as a member of a group. Luckily, I do have supportive friends, friends who don't drink and who are thrilled that I've stopped. And in the past year or so, I started seeing a Jungian therapist, who's been terrific. Jungians love getting into dreams, archetypes. The work I've been doing has given me an incredibly rich perspective about who I am, where I come from, and why I fled to alcohol to escape who I am. In the past five years of sobriety, I've slowly learned that I can go to work, talk to people, have a relatively normal life, one step at a time.

I guess my main revelation is that everyone else is pretty much as lost and confused as I am. Life is one long and courageous ad-lib, a real "hero's journey," as my Jungian therapist would put it. Anyway, that's what I keep seeing, at least when I emerge from my own self-absorption enough so that I *can* see what other people are going through.

One of the ways I calm myself is by taking a walk

down the street and forcing myself to *notice* everyone who passes me. I can't tell you what a trip this is. I also can't tell you how many people walk through the street talking to themselves! It's not just the obviously schizophrenic street people. It's old ladies pulling carts of groceries. Businessmen rushing to beat the traffic light. Students carrying books. When you really look at their faces, you see that they're completely absorbed in their own universes. They're all worrying about deadlines, their health, who loves them, who hates them, how they're going to pay their bills.

I sometimes imagine I can hear these people's inner babble through some kind of magic mental microphone—and boy, is it ever loud! The conversations we all have with ourselves! Everyone's a nut case, really, at least if you define *nut* as someone completely absorbed in his or her own reality. We're all walking around muttering and worrying to ourselves, that's what it seems like to me anyway. But somehow I find this calming. Anything that convinces me "we're all in this together" eases the pressure, makes me feel like *my* little universe isn't the only one. I suppose it's a way of wresting some kind of perspective out of the air. Just look at other people closely enough and you realize everybody's crazy, not just you.

However, Virginia's relationship with Greg has summoned up an anxiety she can't dispel with a walk down the street. "Greg and I met at the library. After I stopped drinking, I discovered that I loved reading. I found Greg—or rather he found me—in the English mystery section. He saw me looking through Josephine Tey titles and informed me that Josephine Tey was, as far as he was concerned, God. He begged me to read *To Love and Be Wise.*" Virginia laughs. "Such a prophetic title. If only I

could 'love and be wise.' " Virginia's smile fades. "It's
that 'ridiculous' thing I talked about. Greg is a *young*
twenty-five. And while I don't look older than I am—
forty-seven—I don't look younger either. You can see my
life in every line in my face. Greg asked me out for coffee
the second time he found me in the mystery stacks. I said
yes although I felt foolish. We talked about Josephine Tey
and somehow got onto the subject of good dim sum
restaurants in Chinatown and then segued improbably
into our favorite movies. In other words, we hit it off. In
fact, I couldn't believe how well we meshed. And I could-
n't believe the sexual spark that was undeniably between
us. My mind told me it was all wrong. But when a spark
like that gets lit, it doesn't care about the mind."

The hardest thing for Virginia to accept is that Greg
truly finds her attractive.

But he does. We had sex after about three months of
dates. You can't fake attraction—you just know it's there
after a while. It's like a tide that comes in when *it* wants
to, according to *its* laws. And Greg obviously loves having sex with me. But I just couldn't—sometimes still
can't—accept it. Sometimes I almost hate Greg for finding me attractive—what does he see in me? Does he have
some kind of weird fixation about older women? I dread
going out to a restaurant with him. I'm sure everyone either thinks I'm his mother or a desperate older woman
with a gigolo. All the wisdom I usually can summon up
about everyone else's self-absorption—which one friend
of mine tells me you should never underestimate—goes
to hell. Whenever I'm with Greg in public, I feel like
we're being scrutinized, judged, and I'm the ridiculous
loser. I feel so ashamed about this that I don't talk about
it with Greg. What I end up doing is confusing him. I'll
cancel most of our dates that put us in crowds. I'll invite

him over for Saturday night dinner and video dates, the following morning cuddling up together over the Sunday papers, but all of it in *private.*

Virginia says that secretly she feels like the beast in *Beauty and the Beast,* "except that in the fairy tale, the beast ends up becoming a beautiful prince. I just keep getting older and more ashamed of keeping this relationship going with Greg." However, this entrenched shame recently got a profound and unexpected jolt.

Greg is normally an easygoing person: he almost always agrees to the boundaries I set up, which, as I've said, mostly have to do with keeping our dates private, not going out in public. But last week, when I said I couldn't go with him to a play he especially wanted to see, he grew uncharacteristically quiet—and cold. He'd never withdrawn like this before. Instantly, my defenses went up; I convinced myself that we'd reached the inevitable moment when he'd tell me our affair was over. I realized then that I'd been steeling myself for this rejection from the first moment I met him. It's as if I almost *wanted* it to happen, so that it would be over with, so that I wouldn't have to feel and deal with all the contradictory emotions being with him brought up in me. It was, I guess, the old alcoholic part of me that would rather just destroy a relationship than deal with its ambiguity, any possibility of uncertainty or pain or rejection. I know from my own experience that an alcoholic's first and last goal is self-protection. And how I've protected myself is generally by getting the hell out of wherever I am at the least sign of trouble. Just because I stopped drinking doesn't mean I've stopped wanting to *escape.* And Greg had become someone, out of my own shame and fear, I secretly *did* want to escape.

"I'm sorry you won't go with me to the play," Greg had said coolly. "But I'm not surprised. You don't seem to want to go anywhere with me." I was struck dumb. All I wanted to do right then was get away from him. I didn't want to explain what the real reason was for my not wanting to be seen with him in public. And I was sure I didn't have to. Surely he didn't want to be seen with me any more than I did. These invitations of his were really a cruel joke. Like he had to keep some sort of ruse up that he didn't mind going out with an older woman. I couldn't accept that he felt any differently. And now his coolness released something I'd held back all through the past year. I started really to hate Greg. He'd just been using me for sex. Some sort of Simone Signoret-older-woman scenario—hadn't he said that one of his favorite movies was *Room at the Top*?

But what Greg said next blew all of these obsessive thoughts apart. "I know I'm not smart or sophisticated enough for you," Virginia quotes Greg as saying. "I know you'd rather be with someone more accomplished, someone's who's *done* something with his life. I often wonder why you have any interest in me at all. And I guess with all of your turn-downs lately, the fact that you won't go anywhere with me, you're trying to let me down easy." Virginia says she was shocked into silence; she never had a clue that Greg felt or thought any of this. Greg evidently interpreted her silence as proof he was right. "You don't know how stupid I feel," he continued. "I'm this complete screwup. I have no idea what I want to do with my life. I feel like I have no talent for anything. I'm just a dilettante. Sure, you humor me by discussing theater and movies and books with me, but you know I'm good-for-nothing. I'm not *going* anywhere. Why would you want to hang around with someone who's not going anywhere?"

Virginia sighs deeply after recounting Greg's confession. "It occurred to me then that Greg and I had never *talked* about what we felt, not only about each other but about ourselves. I had never seen Greg in the light he was sure I had seen him. And I felt like a fool. Here I prided myself on being able to accept everybody else's feelings of fallibility and inadequacy, but I refused to let Greg have the benefit of this wisdom. Greg—young, handsome Greg with all his life ahead of him—was, I thought, exempt from all the fears and doubts that plagued me, that plagued everybody else on the planet. I hadn't allowed for the fact that Greg was *human,* that he had his *own* uncertainties. My own fears had painted a totally inaccurate picture of him. I had never really known him. And I had kept him from knowing me."

Virginia says she found the courage to talk to Greg a little about her own fears, about her inability to believe Greg wasn't somehow disgusted by their age difference. Their conversation quickly became a series of "You mean, you thought *that?*" "*That*'s what you thought I was doing?" "How could you believe . . .?" Their conversation became a series of revelations. They were finally able to begin to share what was really going on behind each of their facades.

While Virginia and Greg have entered a new and deeper stage of closeness, all of her worries about their age difference have not magically been erased. "Nor should they be erased," Virginia says. "I *don't* know that the gap in our experience and ages counts for nothing. I can't really envision us ten, twenty years from now. But I've grown to treasure what Greg and I *do* have right now. And I've learned that I don't have to feel so lonely with him. I think that's what made me hate him, when I did hate him, most of all. Here, physically, we were so intimate, and yet he never really knew what was in my heart and mind. And I never really knew what was in his. Now we know more about that, and now we're simply more careful with each other. We don't cling so steadfastly to our old assumptions. We've learned that sometimes we're both very blind."

Allowing somebody else *in* can feel like a very risky undertaking. But sometimes the people who are already in our lives—Ron and his daughter Marcie, Virginia and Greg—offer us opportunities for contact far greater and deeper than we ever realized. Calling ourselves "alone" is sometimes simple blindness. Often there's somebody else there *already;* we just haven't opened our eyes to see who that someone else is. People who like going to AA meetings often make this discovery: "My God," one friend of mine said recently about his revelation that he actually enjoyed going to his weekly AA meeting, "I actually *like* these people. These people are my friends!" Friendship—a feeling of connection—had sort of sneaked up on him. By simply putting himself in the presence of other people, allowing a kind of intimacy to grow organically over time, he realized he actually cared about the people he saw and that they cared about him. At the right moment of receptivity, he awoke to find that he wasn't as alone or as disconnected as he'd always defined himself before.

The Insidious Nature of Friendship

Intimacy often has a through-the-back-door quality. Again and again I'm struck by the subtle and unpre-

dictable ways our hearts are touched by other people.
The rewards of sobriety seldom come clearly packaged.
But never is this more true than in the ways friendship
evolves, touches us, captures us, connects us.

When I first got sober, I went to a raunchy downtown
New York East Village AA meeting frequented as much
by Bowery bums (who still drank) as it was by people
trying to get sober. I think of this period as golden. I
loved this smelly, dirty place. Physically it linked me with
the mess of my own previous life; it was a sort of halfway
house, a purgatory, between hell and life on earth. The
messages of hope and triumph I heard in this purgatory
had a profound impact on me. It was clear to me that
every single person in the room, bowery bums to aspir-
ing CEOs (who sometimes were the same people), *knew*
what hell was like. Representatives from hell were still all
around us, ready at any moment through a crazed mutter, yelp, or howl to remind us what the disease was that
we were battling. Any triumph that any of us laid claim
to was authentic, wrenched out of the mud by our own
desperate, grasping hands. We each were clawing our
way back to life, and every one of us knew how hard it
was to do that.

Everyone in that vast, dark, messy room seemed to be
put there entirely for my benefit. I saw them all as infinitely fascinating puppets put there for my edification: a
kind of ongoing, funny, outrageous, frightening, touch-
ing morality play staged for me and me alone. However,
in this first year, I remember seeing one "puppet" who
wasn't following the usual script. He was a lean man in
his middle twenties who smoked incessantly. He had a
menacing James Dean sort of attractiveness. Some great
wound had been done to him—that's what I felt when I
looked at him—and he displayed the scars of this wound
defiantly. His lanky, taut muscularity seemed to have de-

veloped to *bear* whatever pain had been inflicted on him. He was tight as a wire. When he spoke, which wasn't often, he was almost frighteningly articulate. He obviously enjoyed throwing verbal grenades: he was no stranger to fights, physical or otherwise. He'd paint quick pictures of his life out on the street, death-defying experiences, hanging off the pier drunk, challenging cops, and getting beaten up, and then, out of nowhere, would come a sudden eruption of tenderness. He'd be quiet and talk about how he loved his brother. Or he'd mention how beautiful the woman he'd seen on the street was, how it broke his heart to see such beauty. But mostly he just sat in the back of the room, smoking, saying nothing, looking sullen.

He was irresistibly enigmatic, and he never seemed to take any notice of me. Through the years, I saw him in and out of meetings, sometimes he'd quit smoking and talk about it—I quit cigarettes around the same time and hung on his every word—sometimes he'd be at the back of the room, silent, cigarette in mouth. I often wondered why he kept coming. He seemed so angry. What were AA meetings doing for him? They didn't seem to be filling him with the usual "gratitude" or elicit from him expressions of great oneness with the world. But I kept seeing him, and the example of his sobriety— he may have gone back to smoking, but he didn't go back to drinking—planted deep roots in me. Somehow, as long as this man was here, sullen and smoking but not drinking, there was hope for me, too. I ached sometimes to talk to him, to have him notice me. But another part of me was glad he kept his iconographic distance. I wasn't sure I wanted him to become more than a symbol, more than a sort of Hollywood metaphor for the angry young (recovering) man.

Years went by. Lovers and changes of job and deaths
of friends and family—this man and I each had our share
of these and talked about them at meetings in our own
very different ways. I was earnest, ebullient, and blither-
ing; he was concise, dark, and pointed. I don't think we
ever exchanged a word privately; we heard each other
only in the context of a meeting. Speaking in an AA
meeting can feel oddly but comfortingly disembodied. It
often strikes me as funny and somehow apt that, after
pouring your heart out about endless doubts and fears
and troubles at a meeting, when somebody walks up to
you later and asks, "How are you?" you say, "Fine." It's
as if all the preceding outpour has spent itself; at that
moment you often *are* "fine." But my James Dean icon
never had this kind of postmeeting small talk with anyone. Not in the five, six, seven years I'd seen him. Somewhere around the eighth year, however, he walked up to
me. I'd been talking about some horror story or other
about a book project. He said he was a writer, too, and
he thanked me for what I'd said in the meeting. Back
home that night, I scoured my memory for what I possibly could have said that moved "James Dean" to thank
me for it. It all had seemed like some blathering and
whining complaint to me. But "James Dean" had talked
to me. This was a heady triumph.

Since that time, "James Dean" and I have spoken
more often, taken the risk of talking to each other with
fewer and fewer inhibitions. We've shown each other our
writing. We've talked about our childhoods. We've
shared the embarrassing emotional details of our lives,
our peccadilloes, our dreams, our dashed expectations,
our desire to step off this whirling planet and have done
with it all. Generally we end up laughing at ourselves.
There is now no one on earth with whom I am more

open about the details of my life. He is no longer "James Dean"; he is a man with his own name and self and as unlike an "icon" as I am. He has turned out to be as complicated and as vulnerable as I know myself to be.

But there is something even more surprising about our relationship. When he is in pain, in the wake of a ruined relationship, in the grip of a black suicidal depression, he calls me. When I am in pain, when I can think of no one in the world to talk to, I call him. (Sometimes I wait for hours, days, weeks, before doing it, but I call him.) We have forged a vital connection. Incredibly, we are *friends*. It is a friendship that has constructed itself. I suppose what surprises me most is that it is so strong, and it means so much to each of us. It is not a relationship based on greed, money, family, competition, or sex. It has no basis other than itself: "we are friends" somehow sums it up, is the last word I know how to put to it. It seems unbelievable to me that I could have let anyone into my life so unselfconsciously and so unconditionally. It seems unbelievable to me that I can accept and give such richness.

Love comes through the back door, through some mysterious osmotic process over which we have very little control. What we can control ultimately is our own blindness and resistance to *seeing* the love that seems, organically, to form in our lives. Some degree of self-acceptance seems to be necessary before this resistance, this blindness, can lift. It was Ron's, Virginia's, and my self-hate and self-absorption that blocked our ability to see the connections that seemed to *want* to happen in our lives. Our impulse, as Virginia tells us, is always toward self-protection, which means to escape any possibility of pain or danger or even ambiguity. Learning to tolerate the unknown seems to be the essential task of anyone who calls him- or herself "recovering."

The rewards of staying in our lives, of not giving into the urge to bolt, are as unexpected as they are nurturing, life-affirming. But the unknown still remains unknown. Fear will continue to assail us. Each of us is, as Virginia's Jungian therapist would tell us, truly on a hero's journey. What we all can learn, however, is that there are other boats in the water, and we can hail one another, make contact, even in the midst of the darkest night or most frightening storm.

Chapter Five

The Other Stuff You Can't Stop Doing

Generally, during the early triage part of recovery—the days, weeks, and months of sober consciousness when it's often all you can do to get out of bed, get through the day, and get back into bed in one piece—your focus is relatively simple. You do what you have to do to live your life without picking up a drink or a drug; everything else takes a backseat. A baby just learning to walk puts a great deal of effort into staying upright. As he toddles along, pretty much all his concentration is on keeping his balance, positioning himself to take his next step. But once the legs get going on their own—and once living sober begins to become more automatic—you become less conscious of the effort it takes to encounter the world on your own two feet. There's more space in your life to focus on—obsess over, worry about, frantically resort to—other behaviors. If you're like the majority of the recovering men and women I've met, it doesn't take long for a lot of other stuff to flood in, and you often butt into other compulsive behaviors besides the one you gave up.

Not all compulsive behaviors are as dangerous as others. You might even benefit from some of the new habitual behaviors that have replaced the old. But you also discover what defines a behavior as bad or good is not always so obvious. Old assumptions often don't hold up.

Most broadly, recovery seems to teach us that behavior is bad when it *impedes* you, when it keeps you from attaining something you want to attain. The bad part of a behavior is rarely the behavior per se; it's the quality of attachment you have to it. Alcohol is deadly to alcoholics not because there's anything intrinsically bad about drinking Beaujolais, Jack Daniels, or Miller Lite. It's the alcoholic's fierce physical, psychological, and emotional *dependence* on alcohol, a dependence that crowds out every other aspect of his or her life, that makes it deadly. It's the same with any other activity. Going to church, visiting your grandmother, or even attending AA meetings might well be something you decide is terrible, self-destructive behavior if you do it so often, fearfully, and obsessively that it blots out the rest of your life.

Of course what most of us find we need to examine aren't our overtly benign behaviors: we need to look at behaviors we've decided are proof that we're "sick," "bad," "weak," "immoral"—ways in which we may turn to sex, food, work, or other substances and activities with the same fierceness and hunger for escape, as well as guilt and shame, that we once turned to drugs or alcohol. What we usually find when we take this look is that automatically damning behaviors conventionally held to be bad isn't any more profitable than automatically condoning behavior conventionally held to be good. Dismissing a behavior as sick, immoral, or shameful almost never helps us to stop the behavior for very long, and it certainly doesn't give us the chance to understand anything about *why* we're resorting to it. We run into so many brick walls when we attack ourselves for being immoral or sick. Automatic judgments like these mean we never give ourselves the chance to *look* at what we're doing, the roots of it, why we cling to it, what it's doing for us, what it may be telling us we *need*.

Perhaps if dismissing a craving or behavior as sick *worked*—if it truly allowed you to give it up and be happier as a result—it might be a profitable option. But it almost never does work. Although you may be able to white-knuckle your way out of a behavior you've labeled sinful, the cost of that white-knuckling is usually that you're more miserable than you ever were before. We do better to respect our hungers rather than harangue ourselves for having them; to try to explore, understand, satisfy, or assuage our cravings (in ways that don't harm us) rather than simply to condemn them.

Greta and Harold have each, in different ways, discovered that the real problem about a compulsive behavior is rarely the behavior—it's their fierce attachment to it. When we hold onto something fiercely, we hold onto it out of fear. If there's a magic key to lessening the hold any compulsive behavior has on us, it seems to be learning to let go of the worst of that fear.

The Pain and Joy of Becoming Visible

Greta, a twenty-six-year-old former model and self-described "recovering pill head and heroin abuser" who says she has battled sex, food, and work compulsions, is very clear about the priority in which she places the cravings that plague her: "I've learned to deal with my addictions in the order in which they'll kill me." It's clear to her, as it is to most of the rest of us, that drugging and drinking kill more quickly and efficiently than most of the other behaviors we may feel compelled to do. "Once I decided I would rather live than die," Greta says, "I stopped doing what most threatened to end my life. In my case, that was diet pills—uppers, amphetamines, anything that would give a jolt of energy and keep me from wanting to eat—and, later, heroin, which did the same thing but didn't make me want to jump out of my skin. God, the *bliss* of heroin—I'd never known anything like that before . . ."

Greta discovered this "bliss" in her early twenties after she'd become a fairly successful photographic model mostly for catalogs but sometimes on the runway for a major designer or two.

I was always skinny as a kid," Greta said, "and not much good at anything they threw at me at school. My parents, both of whom are college professors, had no idea what to do with their daughter who was so totally uninterested in books. I squeaked by in high school, was pretty much of a loner, had only one huge crush, I suppose a typical teenage unrequited love for an older divorced woman in her early forties who taught biology, Mrs. Martin. Yeah, I'm lesbian—maybe that was why I turned off to the world of parents and school. No one I'd met, no one I was supposed to like or look up to or model myself after, held the least interest for me. No one, that is, except Mrs. Martin. I absolutely idolized her. I dreamed about her, about telling her how I felt, about running into her arms. But I kept all those feelings in. I ached to tell this woman how much I loved her, but the greater the ache was, the more guarded I became. What other people saw was a skinny, quiet wallflower. If they'd only known the fantasies burning inside me.

I really had no idea what to do when I got out of high school, and no idea about what to do about these intense feelings for this teacher. I didn't fantasize about women generally—all my longings seemed to concentrate on this one particular woman. I didn't even think of myself as lesbian back then, just obsessed by Mrs. Martin.

After high school, Greta fell into a job as a receptionist in a talent agency: "I applied as a temp—I could type, knew a little Wordperfect—and the first job they put me in was at this agency. The talent they handled mostly meant struggling actors doing commercials and bit parts on TV and models who generally got hired for catalog spreads. God, the desperate faces in the waiting room— sometimes I'm still haunted by them in my dreams. Little did I realize that I'd soon be one of them." Greta became one of them, she says, also "by default. Some model they needed to send out for a small clothes catalog didn't show up. It was an account the agency desperately wanted to keep, and the catalog people would have hit the roof if we hadn't sent somebody in her place. I was still skinny, and I guess better-looking than I realized I was, and the president of the company decided I would do."

Greta's quietness worked in her favor. "I had no idea what to do in that first shoot, but the catalog people were pretty amateurish, too, and they mistook my silence for some sort of sophisticated 'model' disdain or something." Greta laughs. "My father used to tell me that if I ever wanted to seem mysterious and brilliant and enigmatic, just to sit there and say nothing. Everyone will imagine I'm the smartest one in the room! It turned out to be good advice in this instance." Greta turned out to be photogenic, and this job led to others. "The agency decided I was of more use to them in front of a camera than a word processor, and my career as a model began."

What also began was a new and completely unanticipated self-consciousness. "I don't know if I can explain this," Greta says, "but until I became a model, I honestly didn't feel like I existed. It's like I used to think I could erase myself, I could stand in a crowd and *will* people around me not to see me, not to notice me. Now I realize this was a kind of coping mechanism. Whenever anything threatened to overwhelm me, I just mentally checked out. But I really thought I could make myself *invisible,* and for most of my adolescence, I seemed to succeed at it. People didn't notice me much because I made sure not to stand out. But when the camera started clicking . . ." Greta shudders at the memory. "It was like, all of a sudden, I had this *body.* I think most women who want to model are used to showing themselves off, they develop a kind of narcissism—they *want* to be noticed. It's like a drug they can't get enough of. Well, eventually it became something like that for me, too, but not before I scrambled around to get some help for the anxiety I felt, being poked, prodded, and stared at by makeup, wardrobe, and camera people."

The help she found was Valium.

Doctors are easy to get in the modeling world. Everyone has somebody they go to for prescriptions, and I quickly found one who would give me Valium. It calmed me down somewhat, but then I started eating more. Maybe there was some deeper anxiety Valium couldn't reach, I don't know, but I started to eat and, for the first time in my life, gain weight. This was horrifying to me. Being visible as a model was one thing—I mean, as long as you

kept to their height, weight, and measurement requirements you could sort of disappear into the ad—in a way,
I could become invisible by modeling so well that the
clothes were all you noticed. But when I started to gain
weight, I started to stand out—and was quickly given an
ultimatum: either lose the weight or lose the job. I went
back to my Dr. Feelgood, and he started me on diet
pills—amphetamines. God, it was like jumping into a
speeding car. Uppers made me completely crazy. Pretty
soon, I felt like my life was spinning further and further
out of control.

Greta closes her eyes, reliving the "spin," shuddering
slightly again.

I became incredibly absorbed by keeping my weight an
exact one hundred five pounds—that's what I'd determined was the ideal, an ideal that I didn't dare diverge
from. I was anorexic but in a really controlled way. You
see, I somehow *did* manage to keep a realistic view of
what the look was that my employers wanted. I wouldn't
allow myself to turn into a skeleton the way a lot of
anorexic women do. It was more *control:* be the absolute
weight and measurements you had to be, to the fraction
of an ounce, to the centimeter, or else—or else what? I
don't think I ever dared to answer that question. I mean,
partly I was afraid of losing my job. Modeling had become the way I defined myself as well as the way I made
money. But the "or else" was a lot more menacing than
that. There was a much worse horror I was somehow
staving off by keeping to a precise weight. It was unnameable somehow—unspeakable. Anyway, under that
constant self-imposed pressure, I lost the weight, but I
had all this manic energy, and it had nowhere to go ex-

cept back into compulsive measuring and calorie counting. And into being an impatient bitch. Now I looked
okay, but I began to be impossible to be around. Then I
met Katy.

Katy became Greta's first lover. "I was so obsessed
about myself, my weight, my work, that I never noticed
Katy until she literally stopped me in the hall of our
agency one day, took me by the shoulders, and shook
me, peering into my face: 'Hello? When the hell are you
going to notice I've been trying to meet you?' Katy was
nothing if not direct. But she seemed to realize how fragile I was, too. By this time, a good year or two into modeling, I was completely hooked on diet pills, and she'd
had enough experience—I was later to learn, in and out
of bed—with other fragile speeding models to recognize
the signs that I was about to crack. 'Look, honey,' she
said, 'you're fantastically beautiful. But you're going to
shatter into 10 million tiny pieces if you don't wise up.'
Katy had this incredibly strong, persuasive, low, reassuring voice. I felt something when she spoke I hadn't felt
since those days back in high school, mooning over Mrs.
Martin. She certainly got my attention."

Katy was the business manager of the agency, and at
first Greta felt that her interest was entirely commer-
cial—taking care of a valuable commodity. "But I didn't
care. No one had taken such firm charge of me before. I
think, from the first time she opened her mouth, I would
have done anything she told me to." One of the first
things Katy said to Greta was that there was an alterna-
tive to uppers. A model didn't have to go nuts to keep her
weight down. In fact, there was a much more pleasurable
way . . .

"Heroin has such a rep, like those old movies they

used to show in school, how it starts with cigarettes, then beer, then you move to marijuana, then down the line where you were completely doomed, out of control, you got to hell: heroin. But when Katy suggested that I try some, that it would not only help me keep my weight down, but make me feel good in the bargain, not so crazed and driven, and that most of the successful models she worked with did heroin and didn't become addicted—they just took it like medicine, with complete control—she sounded so reasonable that I decided I would try it."

That first night—Katy invited Greta to stay in her apartment so that she wouldn't be alone the first time she shot up—was, Greta says, "one of the most incredible experiences I've had in my life." Katy not only administered the heroin—"the sting of the needle going into my arm almost felt good, like some kind of necessary, longed-for initiation," Greta says—but she administered more tender loving care than Greta ever expected. "She slowly unbuttoned my shirt, slipped it off me, so slowly and sweetly, like a mother with a child . . . then helped me wriggle out of my jeans . . . then dangled her soft hair in my face and bent down to kiss me." Greta sighs. "I had never experienced such complete bliss in my life. As the heroin took effect, it was like all the cares I'd ever had in my life lifted one by one, like petals blown off a flower into the air. And then, as Katy began to caress me, make love to me, it was like—well, there aren't words for what it was like. I hadn't dreamed, even back when I yearned for Mrs. Martin, that anything physical could be so completely satisfying. It was like every last fiber of me was touched, softly, with pleasure . . ."

Discovering sex and heroin on the same night made this, Greta says, one of her life's most potent rites of passage. "But—well, while there were other nights like that one, never as completely delicious as that one, but pretty damned wonderful—the rest of the story is pretty simple and sordid and all too easy to tell. I got as hooked on heroin as I had been on uppers. I started nodding out at modeling assignments. I started turning down summer clothes ads because my arms had tracks on them. Worse, Katy began to ignore me and turn her attention to the next new 'tense' model, whom she 'relaxed' in the same way she'd relaxed me. In other words, very quickly, within, I'd say, six to eight months, I was a heroin addict, unemployed, and suicidally depressed."

Greta doesn't exactly know why she decided to stop doing heroin and seek help. "It had something to do with Katy, I guess. I mean, I'd somehow mixed sex and Katy and heroin and modeling and even memories of Mrs. Martin all into the same roiling pot. It was like all of these people, yearnings, disappointments, unfulfilled promises of pleasure, all of it became this mess I couldn't get out of my mind and yet wanted desperately to escape. I really wanted to go back to my invisibility, that quiet, nothing little girl that could flit into the cracks and escape. Whenever I did heroin, I'd get to that blissful feeling for a while, but quicker and quicker, I'd start to emerge back into the black feelings again—heroin was like a chemical Katy—and somehow it hit me that if I wanted to escape Katy and the whole world I was in with Katy, I'd have to stop doing heroin. I don't know what to say other than I was *sick* of it—sick of the wooziness, the sordidness of my life. I wanted *out*. It's funny, the same desire to escape that *drew* me to drugs is what got me out of them."

Greta appeared, unannounced, at her parents' doorstep. She hadn't been in touch with them much in the past few years; now, numb, knowing that she needed to get into some kind of treatment very quickly, she told

them an abbreviated story of what her life had become
and asked them to help. "They were great. They didn't
even blink at the lesbian parts. Right then and there,
they simply drove me to a hospital they knew had a good
rehab. And they put me in it." Greta has been clean for
two years. "I decided I didn't want to do methadone any
more than I wanted to do heroin. I went through a su-
pervised hellish withdrawal that lasted a little less than a
week. And, I don't know, I must have been ready or
something, but I don't miss heroin one bit. It's like some
great black blanket I finally managed to take off me."

But the urge to be "blanketed" hasn't gone away.

I go to this group therapy thing at the outpatient clinic
associated with the rehab I went to. A woman I met there
turned me on to a Narcotics Anonymous meeting for
women only. Between those two places, I've actually
learned to connect with people I'd call friends now. Not
only friends—lovers, too. In fact, too many lovers. It's
like whatever desire I felt so fiercely back in high school
for Mrs. Martin, whatever that complete feeling of bliss
was I'd known with Katy—*that* was closer to what I'm
looking for than heroin. And in the past year or so, I've
had endless serial affairs—hanging out at lesbian coffee-
houses, falling in love with one woman after another, going to bed with one woman after another. As isolated as
I once felt, as much as I never acknowledged that I was
lesbian, but rather that I was just entranced by a particular woman, well, to that same degree, now I want *every*
woman I meet, now all I *am* is lesbian.

Women aren't supposed to be like this. We're supposed to want to merge and stay with one partner, aren't
we? Gay men are supposed to be the anonymous preda-
tors. But I want both. I want to merge emotionally *and* I
want as many fabulous blissful moments of sexual con-

nection as I can get with as many women as I can find. As much as I couldn't get enough amphetamines and then heroin before, now I can't get enough contact with other women. I try to tell myself it's just because I'd felt so alone, so isolated, so abnormal, so *un*touched, for all those years that I'm trying to make up for lost time. But I know, kind of, that the hole I want to fill isn't fillable. There isn't enough love in the world to fill it. All there is is momentary satisfaction. And of course, when you're hooked to people instead of drugs, you get the whole load of wash with it. Oh, the weariness of being involved with people! The jealousies, resentments, the boredom, the lies, the desperate reassurances, the fights—why is none of this ever, ever easy?

But recently, Greta has come to a glimmer of understanding about why she's been so desperate to escape into sex and love or anything else. "I was on welfare for the first year and a half after I got off heroin," Greta says,

Which gave me a lot of time to get involved in everybody else's life. But about five months ago, I got a job working at an outreach clinic that works with homeless women, offering them food and health care and advice about how to navigate the welfare system. The people in the street you pass without thinking they're human—well, they *are* human, they all have lives and pasts, and some of them have a good deal of wisdom. Of course, some of them are just sad schizophrenics or brain-damaged alcoholics. But I guess the biggest overall revelation I've had is that almost every woman who walks into the clinic feels as invisible as I used to feel—sometimes still do feel. They come up to you expecting absolutely nothing, almost willing themselves to get nothing. They have, many of them, such an investment in *being* invisible.

And I really got something about my own past, my own attempts to erase myself. Although I wasn't conscious of it, for most of my life I must have felt I had only two choices: either to pretend I didn't exist, and therefore become able to ignore the gaping hole of need in the center of me, or acknowledge that I did exist, which meant spend every waking moment feeling that need, desperately seeking to fill that unfillable hole. Given that choice, who wouldn't opt for invisibility, for blankness, for mindlessness? And then this drunken little old lady walks up to the table I'm sitting at, where I'm handing out bag lunches. She's a real wino—smells like she steeps herself in it—and she's muttering, I can barely make out the words, but it's obviously a monologue she's kept going for years, something like, "I'm so cold, my skin is so thin, people don't realize I just don't have the skin for life, I don't have that extra layer that everybody has, it's harder for me, that's all, it's just harder because it's so cold, and I don't have the skin for it . . ."

Something, Greta says, suddenly became clear.

I felt *I* didn't have that extra layer either, "the skin for life." This little old lady had put into words something I'd never been able to articulate. The reason I tried so desperately to escape being visible, tried so desperately to become the perfect model, tried so desperately to stay in the deep bliss of heroin and sex with Katy, tried so desperately to lose myself in love affair after love affair in sobriety, and recently have tried so desperately to fill myself with chocolate mint Oreos—yeah, I'm gaining weight again—is somehow to provide myself with that extra layer, that thicker skin, that everyone else seems to have. I guess I'm just acknowledging that I *feel* things very intensely, and I've been scared stiff of feeling them.

I've brought this idea up in my various groups, and it's gotten other women to talk about their own feelings of "skinlessness." I'm obviously not the only one who feels this way.

The problem is, we've always seen this intense sensitivity as an affliction—for obvious reasons. Things just *hurt* more when you lack that skin. But it's also a gift, isn't it? To feel this intensely? I mean, it also means that you feel joy and pleasure more intensely, not just pain. Anyway, I'm starting to see that maybe I have more choices than to erase myself or throw myself into a bottomless pit of need. Maybe I can *survive* up here at the surface, being careful of this thin skin, but learning that I can live in it. I know I'm probably not making this very clear—hell, it's not really clear to me. But somehow I'm starting to be able to sort out that unfillable hole, the one that goes back to infancy probably, from the *fillable* holes in my life. Maybe I don't have to turn to every woman I meet for the "final solution"—to make me feel safe and complete and whole for the rest of all time. Maybe just accepting the love they can give, the love I can give back, maybe just accepting the limitations of loving and receiving love when you've got a thin skin. Anyway, I'm starting to entertain the idea that there may be satisfactions I can enjoy, a visible self I can trot out, without quaking in fear or escaping to some intense sensation. Not that this idea that I might be able to survive being who I am, incomplete, unfilled, uncertain, still prey to fear and anxiety, makes me feel riotously joyful or anything. I mean, that unfillable hole in the center of me *is,* as far as I can make out, unfillable. Accepting that some kind of emptiness, some basic feeling of disconnectedness is part of life isn't easy when you're terrified of *any* emptiness.

But, I don't know, it might just be the contrast to the

homeless women I see at the clinic who are still so afraid, who try so hard to stay invisible, but I'm starting to feel like I can *be* visible, like I can stand up and count for something—even if I'm imperfect or incomplete. I'm even sort of looking forward to being a little fat. I'm beginning to like the idea of being able to pinch some flesh around my starving middle.

Showdown with "the Beast"

The forbidding "or else" Greta spoke of that kept her diving compulsively into one behavior after another, the "unnameable, unspeakable" horror she felt she was staving off through all of her desperate escape tactics, describe feelings that resonate with most of the recovering addicts and alcoholics. Harold, a forty-five-year-old assistant principal of a large suburban junior high school, says that he too feels trailed by some "black shadow." "I always feel if I stop being vigilant for even one second, something terrible, like some kind of terrible beast, will pounce on me. Or if something good happens, it has to be followed by something disastrous. It's really a sort of paranoia, I guess. And I don't know where it comes from. I mean, I had a stable enough childhood; it's not like my parents beat me or abandoned me or anything like that. I can't remember any time in childhood ever being afraid of the bogeyman, or of snakes or crocodiles under the bed, or of the dark . . ." He pauses. "Not true. I was terrified of the dark. Had to have a nightlight by the bed—screamed for that until I got it." Harold frowns and shakes his head slowly. "But the real problem started after I stopped drinking. That's when I became aware of trying to escape whatever this 'beast' is I think is trailing me."

Harold quit drinking because his wife gave him an ultimatum: either stop drinking or divorce her.

I got married late—I was forty-two. I'd really given up on the idea of finding anyone I could live with, which means love enough to live with. But Karen was different. I really do love my wife, and I was shocked to hell that she thought my drinking was getting in the way of our marriage. I mean, I limited myself to three or four drinks in a friendly bar around the corner after work—a town far from the one where I'm a principal, so there was no chance of students or colleagues seeing me there—and then had maybe two more drinks before dinner at home and several others afterward. Well, I realize now that I was a drunk all right, but because I seemed to be able to keep functioning as a good principal and administrator, I couldn't imagine that I had a problem.

So when my wife staged her little intervention—not an official one with a shrink or anything, but just as effective—it blew me away. She said that I'd been slipping further and further away, that there wasn't a night I didn't pass out, that the only time she saw me sober was in the morning before going to school, and that just wasn't enough. She was living with the shell of a man, she said, and it not only broke her heart to see me sinking like this, but it had made her own life too empty to continue. My wife never nagged at me, so when she staged this confrontation a year into our marriage, I wasn't in any way prepared for it. Like I said, it blew me away.

Harold managed to stop drinking on his own. "Recently, just in the past six months, I've dropped into a lo-

cal AA meeting, sat in the back, listened, and sort of enjoyed the proceedings, but I'm still undecided about
whether or not to continue with meetings or how much
to get involved. I understand the idea about having support. It's just that my wife has given me so much support,
she was so thrilled when I stopped drinking, that I didn't
feel the need to go outside for any more. Until recently,
that is."

Recently, Harold gave up two other activities, only
one of which his wife knew about. Harold names them:

Food and sleeping pills. Karen certainly knows about the
food, but she never had a clue about the sleeping pills.
But both are connected; they both go back to the anxiety
I felt the first days I stopped drinking. It's just this: I
found I simply couldn't go to sleep when I stopped drinking. I had depended for so many years on alcohol to
knock me out, I had no idea what it was like to go to
sleep without it. The first couple of nights after I quit, I
tossed and turned, had anxiety attacks, felt like I was in
a waking nightmare—it was horrible. It was then that
this feeling hit me that something dreadful was following
me; some sort of dark presence was tailing me, waiting
for me around every corner. I guess I must have dozed
here and there for a few minutes, but for those first couple of nights, I went through hours and hours in a state
of horrible anxiety, an anxiety that rose and fell in
waves, an anxiety over which I seemed to have absolutely
no control. I've put it together now that part of this was
simple physical withdrawal from alcohol. But there was
something emotional going on, too. I guess I just didn't
realize how much a *medication* drinking had been for
me; it had sort of lopped off at the root any anxiety I'd
ever had in the past, cut it off before it had a chance to

get going. But now it was growing like a wild cancer—and I couldn't escape it. I really felt I was going crazy.

Harold secretly saw a doctor three days after he stopped drinking and persuaded him to prescribe some strong sleeping pills. "The fact that I kept this secret from Karen should have given me a clue that I didn't feel good about it," Harold says. "I obviously felt I was doing something evil or wrong." He kept the bottle in his locked desk at school, taking only one or two tablets home a day, which he kept hidden in his pocket until about a half hour before bedtime, when he locked himself in the bathroom, brushed his teeth, "got ready for bed," and gulped the pills down. "I was so paranoid about Karen somehow finding out," Harold says, "that sometimes when I'd gulp the pills down I'd choke on them—I don't know what I thought would happen, that Karen would suddenly decide to kick the locked door in? But the point is, I was afraid. I didn't want Karen to know that I was "cheating," taking pills now instead of drinking."

What Karen couldn't escape noticing was Harold's weight gain. "The sleeping pills helped me to get through the night, but I also had to get through the day," Harold explains. "I discovered that with enough carbohydrates and fat from Dunkin' Donuts, Burger King, and Pizza Hut, I could still "medicate" myself, keep my anxiety somewhat at bay. In six months, I gained sixty pounds. Alcohol turned out to be a pretty tough act to follow—I mean, it took two or three nightly sleeping pills and about four thousand calories a day of junk food to replace it. But replace it I did."

Had the junk food and the sleeping pills continued to work, Harold doubts he would have considered stopping either. But, he says, "after a year or so, the anxiety kept coming back, sort of seeping through when I didn't expect it. I had odd, disjointed panic attacks during the day—wondering if I'd accidently left one of my pills on the sink so that Karen would find it, imagining that various teachers at the school were criticizing me behind my back. Before long, there were a dozen, a hundred, a thousand tiny moments during the day when this anxiety would prick me. And I'd eat more. And I'd experiment with taking more sleeping pills, sometimes taking one in the early afternoon to see if it would calm me down. Karen noticed more than my weight gain. As the weeks grew into months and then into a year, she'd try to get me to talk about what was obviously bothering me. But I wouldn't know what to say. And I mean I literally wouldn't have a clue about how to tell her—or myself—what was slowly eating me alive. The only thing I knew how to do was keep eating and keep medicating myself at night—and, as I've said, sometimes during the day. I was this fat, sweating, nervous man, getting fatter, damper, and more nervous as the days went on."

Recently, the sleeping pills Harold took during the day knocked him out in his office.

Thank God, it was during lunch, followed by a school-wide assembly that I didn't have to be at, so nobody found me asleep on my desk. But when I groggily came to about two-thirty in the afternoon and realized that I'd once again made myself pass out, I felt such a jolt of revulsion, such a sledgehammer of self-hate, that I could barely breathe. What was becoming of me? I was now a drug addict—that's what this amounted to! It wasn't fair to Karen. It wasn't fair to all the people who depended on me at school. And I suppose, somewhere dimly in there, I knew it wasn't fair to me. But I hated myself so much that I barely gave myself the right to feel I counted for anything. All I knew right at that moment was that I had to get rid of the sleeping pills. I took the bottle to the lavatory and flushed its contents down the toilet. For that moment, I felt the first flutter of relief I think I'd felt—since when? I think it was the first relief I'd *ever* felt in my life. I didn't feel relieved when I stopped drinking—I went into a state of panic. And for years before that, years before I even knew Karen, I'd only been able to navigate the world with alcohol. Somehow the act of pouring those pills down the toilet was the first tiny indication that something like relief was even possible.

But this tiny moment of relief quickly passed. "I went through the rest of the day, got into the car to go home, didn't stop at Dunkin' Donuts, which was my usual habit, and was determined to see Karen in as sober a state as I could manage." Harold said he went through the early evening quietly. "I didn't say much. It's like I was trying out this new reality without my usual buffers, without the expectation that I'd knock myself out to go to sleep or keep myself medicated with food the next day. I don't know that Karen noticed anything different, except that I was quieter than usual. We watched our usual television programs—I remember it was a Friday night. No school the next day, which didn't make me feel either good or bad. At about eleven, Karen kissed me and said she was going to bed. I said good night and told her I'd follow in a little while."

But Harold couldn't follow her.

Suddenly, out of nowhere, I had this tremendous feeling of dread. It was like the black thing I'd been trying to escape for years was now ready to pounce. I could no longer hold it off. I had no *power* to hold anything off.

For some reason I started reviewing my whole life—way back into childhood, up through high school and college, my decision to become a teacher, my promotion to being a principal. All I could see was this child running from one hope of security to another, one hope after another proving inadequate. *There was no escape*—there never had been. It was no coincidence that I was working in a junior high school. In some ways I was still about twelve or thirteen. I realized there had never been a time in my life when my schedule was not dictated by the school year. As I looked over each desperate move I'd made in my life, everything seemed exposed as a sham— as pathetic attempts to escape, to find some job or role to lose myself in, all of it evidence that I was incapable of really taking care of myself. Karen had talked about having kids. She was still in her thirties, but she felt her biological clock ticking. I kept encouraging us to hold off. Kids? *I* was the kid. How could I take care of any?

As Harold's anxieties crept up and intensified, he said, "I just felt frozen; I couldn't move out of the chair. Karen had evidently fallen asleep already, maybe had no idea I was still in the living room, unable to move. No one knew where I was, how I felt. Finally I was able to get my hand to reach out for the remote control of the television. I thought maybe the mindless boob tube would help me to escape. Then it hit me like a ton of bricks that *I had no sleeping pills*. There would be no escape tonight. I wondered what was in the kitchen that I might gorge on. But I couldn't get out of my chair. I couldn't even push the power button on the remote. It was like, whatever horrible confrontation I was holding off, I was doomed to have to go through this night."

Minutes ticked by, Harold was bolt upright awake in

his chair, waiting for something—whatever the "beast" was—to take him over. Minutes crept into hours. Harold said he sometimes tried to focus on turning on the television, but the remote remained inert in his hand. "I knew I'd never be able to sleep. Every tiny creak of the house tortured me. How was anyone ever able to sleep? The world was so uninviting, so damned noisy and chaotic! I couldn't imagine why I'd ever gotten married. Why would Karen ever have agreed to marry someone as flawed as I was, someone as ill equipped as I was to deal with anything? I steeled myself: whatever I would have to go through, I knew now there was no escaping it. By degrees, I felt I was turning to stone—numb more than panicked."

Somewhere around four or five in the morning, Harold realized that the numbness had slowly turned into something else. He realized he'd *given in* to not being able to sleep.

It was strange. Once I actually accepted that I was going to be awake all night, once I accepted that it was *all right* to be awake all night, something started to soften in me. I wasn't as afraid. I'd sat in the living room chair for hours and hours and no beast had come. I had the sudden strange desire to get up, to walk toward the door, open it, go out on the porch, sit on the step, and watch the sun come up. What a strange feeling this was! There was something *light* about it. It no longer seemed impossible to move. So I did get up, I did quietly pad out to the porch. And I sat down on the step and looked into the sky. The air was cool and damp, almost refreshing. What a strange, silent world it was just before dawn! It's like I was the only one awake in the world. I looked over to other sleeping houses. I'd been given a *gift*, this aware-

ness, this *seeing* something that no one else could see. I
began to feel almost happy.

The eastern sky grew faintly light, then pink. I understood, softly now, the panic had gone, that the great
black thing I'd been running from all my life—well, there
was no "great black thing." What happens is, morning
comes. The sun rises. No one has a gun to my head. I realized I'd always seen my life as obligatory—something I
had to do, something I needed to get a passing grade on,
just like the kids in my school, something I was driven to
do to keep myself safe and approved of. Now I got a
strange message: it was all chosen! Even the things I
thought weren't choices turned out to be choices—in my
life, mostly made out of fear, but choices nonetheless. I
began to wonder what it would be like *not* to choose out
of fear. Suddenly I felt tired, unspeakably tired. More exhausted than I could ever remember being. And being
exhausted was a relief—a pleasure even. I was feeling it
without fear. I was feeling *something* without fear. It was
the first time in my life I could say that. Dimly, as I got up
to go to bed, I wondered what I might have for breakfast
when I decided to wake up. Breakfast seemed like a wonderful idea. I could actually choose what to eat if I
wanted. I considered my options without fear. How the
options began to glow, how pleasant, how promising
they seemed!

Harold laughs at the memory. "I know I was exhausted. I mean, when the prospect of pancakes versus
scrambled eggs begins to seem like a spiritual awakening . . . well, I was a little dopey from lack of sleep. But
something took root on this night. It was simple: I discovered I could get through the night without escaping
it. I could *be*. That was the discovery. And it created a
feeling in me, a palpable feeling, that I've now come to

trust I can feel again. I know now what it's like not to be afraid. And this seems to be the one thing that saves me—this understanding that I don't have to be afraid."

In the past few weeks, Harold has begun to talk to Karen more openly about his fears, which, despite his revelation that he doesn't need them, still sometimes rush in and smack him silly. "I haven't told her about the sleeping pills because, I don't know, I guess I came to my own peace about that. But we've begun working out some sort of food regimen where I don't pig out as much. And, like I've said, I've started to sit in on some AA meetings, although I don't know what I'll do about them in the long run. I'm even thinking of seeing a therapist at some point. But the main big difference is that there now really do seem to be options. Some door has opened a crack. There is now at least a little light where before, I realize, there had been absolutely none."

Accepting Impulses: A Growing Comfort with Being Who You Are

The compassion that Harold and Greta have learned to feel about their own fearful motives has led them each to a new and healing self-knowledge. Greta grabs less desperately for love as she sees and respects her own ache to be "seen" and discovers that she doesn't need sexual approval to define herself. Harold has discovered he can survive the night—both the literal night and the symbolic "black beast" night—without hammering himself into unconsciousness. He doesn't need to protect himself so fiercely against some imagined enemy: he can "be" without the buffers he once thought he needed to survive. By their example, we see that self-knowledge also encour-

ages an ultimately stronger sense of *self,* a self that can
choose what it wants more playfully, more discerningly,
more wisely, a self that can tolerate lapses back into old
fears, the "mistakes" of clinging compulsively once
again to something or someone, a self that can learn
from inevitable setbacks and redress the balance, continue to live, and choose to live, freely, passionately.

Sometimes, when our senses of self have strengthened
sufficiently, we even discover that we can choose behavior we'd once dismissed as sinful without harming ourselves. Mike eventually discovered that, even if he
wanted to, he couldn't will his sadomasochistic sexual
fantasies away; he discovered it didn't make sense to try.
What he *could* do was look at them, examine them,
learn from them. As he got stronger and more capable of
choice, he found he could even play around with them a
little, allow them a place in his life, and still emerge psychically intact. But the greater sense of permission we
can gain is not, of course, limited to sex. Once our core
conscious selves, our egos, begin to function with more
strength and freedom, so many choices in every area of
our lives become possible.

We seem to strengthen that core self by learning not to
run away from our feelings, by learning to withhold automatic judgments that slam the door shut on "objectionable" topics. Once again, we learn that the world is a
much larger, more abundant, and surprising place than
we realized it was when we started on the road to recovery. But we also strengthen this core self by giving ourselves permission to fall down, to take false steps, make
incomplete stabs at things, be clumsy, try out new atti-
tudes and behaviors. One thing we need to make peace
with is that the impulse to seek some cure-all (what
Greta called a "final solution") is probably never going
to go away. Compulsive behaviors are often like bumps

in the rug—push one down here, it's guaranteed to pop up over there. But we needn't see these bumps as afflictions—evidence that we're pathologically needy. The creature that causes these bumps to form is something very precious. It's the *seeking* part of ourselves that we need to respect, take care of, love. We need to *encourage* this "seeking," give it space, not slap it down every time it appears to be getting too compulsive.

In an interesting and often quoted letter from Carl Jung to AA cofounder Bill Wilson, Jung makes the connection between human "spirit" and the "spirits" we call alcohol: "alcohol in Latin is *spiritus* and you use the same word for the highest religious experience as well as for the most depraving poison." Recovering people usually discover that the motive to "escape" through alcohol or drugs is closely linked to the motive to seek the "escape" of *enlightenment* in sobriety. The difference is that one means of escape (drugs and alcohol) blots out consciousness and eventually kills us; the other means of escape (the human-spirit kind) promotes consciousness, leads to life. But one thing seems guaranteed: for whatever nature-and-nurture reasons, whether or not we drink and drug, whatever search we pursue, we will probably always have the impulse to go overboard, to take things to extremes. And this isn't always a bad thing. In fact, sometimes it's a very wonderful thing.

In Search of the Passionate Sober Life: My Edwardian Bordello

My apartment is a potent and, to me, endlessly instructive example of my own "will to excess." My shorthand description of it is "Edwardian bordello." In the nearly three years I've inhabited this tiny Greenwich Village studio—basically one room with a kitchen you can just about make toast and coffee in—I have turned it into a precise physical manifestation and reflection of my psyche. It's sort of my "Id on Parade": densely packed, draped, layers on layers, with burgundy, velvet, brass, candles, silk ropes upon silk ropes, beads hanging off a damasked table, framed and flaking nineteenth-century photographs, prints, hanging glass ornaments, pillows, fake Tiffany lamps, and books, piles of them, stacks of them, filling a wall of shelves, I've even got dried roses and a gilded plaster angel (playing the violin) on top of my computer printer—all a sort of defiant middle finger raised to the twentieth century. From one point of view, it's totally out of control. From the point of view I would rather take, it's the thrilling childlike expression of my psyche, *writ large*. My obsessions and passions, which range from 1959 General Motors cars to London to boxing, are everywhere in various two- and three-dimensional representations, hanging from the ceiling, piled on the floor, and all over the walls. Everything I am has distilled out of me, been compulsively made manifest.

All of the desperation that used to send me into bars every day of my drinking life has found an outlet here. It is my crib. I will sit on my draped couch, staring at the mantelpiece in the morning light, envision yet another lyrical line of rope or beading or branch, and head out the door right then and there, no matter the time or the weather or generally what else I have to do, in search of the missing necessary part. I'm completely compulsive about it. But the compulsion is in service of something so joyous and so important to me that I revel in it. I will go—and already nearly have gone—to the ends of the earth to satisfy it.

Not that it doesn't get dangerously out of hand some-times. When I find myself up to my ears in credit card debt, worrying about where the next tax payment is go-ing to come from, wondering how I'm going to get through the year, it does occur to me that the money spent on custom framing and the damask tablecloth might better have gone elsewhere. I learn and relearn the same lesson: just because my "compulsiveness" serves my urge to manifest all over my walls (however noble that urge may be), it doesn't mean that I always ought to give in to it. Sometimes you have to pay the rent. I have to bring the same vigilant attempts to be conscious about how I spend my money in flea markets as I did, and do, about renewing my pact not to drink.

My point is simply this: the "other stuff" we do be-sides drinking or drugging is often—perhaps always—evidence of a volcanic life urge in each of us, a life urge to be cherished and welcomed, an eruptive force that com-pels each one of us to *be* as fully as we can be. Harness-ing that force takes incredible vigilance, as we all know from our own war stories about getting sober and our war stories about dealing with sex, food, work, and other channels through which our "vulcanism" some-times courses out of control—as I know every time I see a new brass candlestick and have to hold myself back.

But sometimes you *don't* have to hold yourself back. Sometimes it's a terrific idea to buy the candlestick or have imaginative sex or eat that incredible hot fudge sun-dae or work yourself silly over the weekend because you can't wait to see what the chair you're building is going to look like. And, of course, sometimes doing any or all of the above *doesn't* work; sometimes it gets scarily out of control, and you feel like you're slipping back into an obsessional hell—it's just not working, not even the stuff you thought you "loved." Sometimes you're merely disappointed or bored. Anything can happen: joy doesn't always come on cue or when we want it to. But you can recover and go on from both joy and misery. Neither need capsize you.

Whatever happens when we follow our impulses, it seems to me we have to *accept* them, our desires to "let-'er-rip," our urges to go as far as we can go into whatever route it seems urgent to us to take—accept and celebrate them. Sometimes we need to ride the pendulum to its fullest swing. What we learn, through an untold number of trials and errors, is what will kill us and what won't. Then we try to choose the latter.

Moderation is an awfully tepid, unpalatable goal. *Balance* is the worthy pursuit. Not a white-knuckled moderation that strangles life and keeps you from doing the passionate work or play you yearn to do. Being sober isn't a matter of not being passionate. It's a matter of being who you are without killing yourself. Sometimes that means walking a tight rope. Just remember: tight ropes are a lot easier to walk when you're not bombed out of your mind. Or as one friend of mine with over twenty years of sobriety always says to me when I ask him for advice: "Stay sober. Then do whatever the hell else you want to do."

Chapter Six

Finding Yourself Wherever You Go: Life After Relapse

The admonition with which I ended the last chapter may sound pretty reckless. But it's the experience of all the recovering addicts and alcoholics I know that as long as you're able to maintain the first part ("Stay sober"), the second part ("Then do whatever the hell else you want to do") can't help but promise some adventure, reward, or at least illumination. By staying sober, you're making a commitment to stay alive and conscious. Anything you do in that state will have some kind of payback (even if it's only the realization that you never want to do it again). You *learn* when you're conscious: everything you do becomes, or has the potential of becoming, a kind of useful education.

But what if you don't stay sober? What if it feels like you *can't* stay sober?

Relapse is a forbidding demon to so many of us in recovery. We're often told some frightening things about it, that we may never come back if we "go out" again, that our alcoholism or drug addiction progresses whether or not we're drinking or drugging so that if we pick up again, it will be as if we'd never stopped. We'll suffer a much more profound degradation than we knew the last time. I've certainly met enough people who subscribe to Twelve-Step programs who understand that you *can* come back after slipping and that not all of these dire warnings are warranted, but AA and NA do nonetheless seem to be the sources for a lot of this doom-speak.

Of course, some degree of doom-speak may be appropriate: dire warnings have their uses. Perhaps the strongest mission in this book is to encourage you to do whatever it takes to be *conscious*—my synonym for *sober.* As we saw with Len and his drill-sergeant sponsor, sometimes you have to go to great lengths to put a lid on behavior that gets you into trouble: staying away from bars, drug contacts, or other people who drink or use drugs; working your AA or NA program if you're in a Twelve-Step group; going to meetings (of whatever therapeutic stripe) regularly, even every day; and generally *forcing* yourself to keep your hand off the substances that were destroying you. You may well need a drill sergeant of an AA sponsor or a therapist or a superego to keep you from throwing yourself off a cliff.

But ultimately the power behind this discipline has to come from you—your own motivation. You have to be convinced that this path (whether straight and narrow or wildly permissive) is serving you, your deepest desires. If the hundreds of men and women I have talked to—many of whom have relapsed one, two, three, or many more times and come back—have taught me anything, it's that we only become conscious or sober out of *desire* for it, not out of imposing something that only feels like a deprivation or a prison sentence. A basic psychological fact that probably applies more vividly to alcoholics and addicts than to any other broad category of people is simply this: we move toward pleasure and away from pain. This means that sobriety has to be something you *want* for you to pursue it.

It is my contention that all of us *do* ultimately want to be sober in the sense of sober consciousness that has emerged in the stories of this book. Consciousness turns out to offer rich pleasures, connections, and insights, which we slowly learn to savor as we take the time to inhabit sobriety. But sometimes it can take a good deal of time before we decide that sober consciousness *is* a pleasure. Many of us are on a second, third, or ninth try at sobriety, hopping back and forth over both sides of the fence about the merits of unaltered consciousness.

What do we learn from hopping back and forth? At the very least, you'll discover that, no matter what you may have heard to the contrary, you always do have the option to return to the sober side of the fence. But you will also discover something more: you take yourself wherever you go, whatever side you end up on. All the addicts and alcoholics I've met who decide to re-root themselves in sober soil have done so at least partly because they realized they couldn't escape who they were, even through drinking and drugging. It finally became less exhausting to stop *trying* to escape who they were than to keep up the fruitless chase. That's really the beginning of anyone's sobriety: deciding, finally, after years of avoiding the confrontation, to meet yourself without bolting away.

Breaking a Sensual Rut

"At the risk of stating the obvious," Lawrence says, stirring a packet of raw sugar into his cappuccino, "I drank because it felt good. In fact," Lawrence continued, "I'd say that I do everything in my life because it feels good. Hell, look what I'm doing right now. I like feeling a little jolt of caffeine, I like the feel and look of the soft froth of a cappuccino, I like a touch of *real* sweetness—please, no chemical-tasting substitutes! I even like the way these transparent amber crystals of sugar look—that's part of the reason I use them. Beauty and pleasure dictate my life. I can be stopped dead in the street by the sight of a woman I find desirable. I can stare for hours out the window at the twisted lyrical shape of a certain Japanese maple. All of this beauty seeking doesn't change whether or not I'm sober. In fact, when I chose to drink, it was because the letting go that alcohol can give me just allowed me to enjoy my life more. You have to let go to *see* pleasure, feel it, have it. Anything that will help me to do that, I'll do. I'm an unapologetic sensualist—always have been, probably always will be."

However, Lawrence's pursuit of pleasure has, he admits, deposited him at a number of dead ends. "Because of an inheritance from my grandmother—not huge, but it pays the rent and some of my expenses—I've been able to indulge my passions more than the average guy. I'm a painter, I sell some stuff—there are a few galleries nearby at various New England villages and resorts that carry my work—but mostly I do it for myself. I suppose I've done everything for myself. At least that's what my latest woman friend Louise made clear to me."

Although he's never married, Lawrence, at fifty-two,

has nonetheless been involved in the lives of many women, most of whom, he says,

> Finally get tired of playing second fiddle to my easel and more generally not being able to get me to commit. I suppose I've always been one of those Peter Pan types—the little boy who can't or won't grow up. I used to lie more. I mean, I used to tell whatever woman I was with that, yes, I really did want to marry someday, I really did want a family, to settle down, to have that whole part of the American dream, and sometimes, especially with the help of Cutty Sark or a good Bordeaux, I convinced myself that I *did* want that kind of life. But more deeply, I never have. And I kept disappointing woman after woman.
>
> By the time I was in my forties, nobody really believed I'd ever give up my bachelorhood, and in one sense it's been easier. I sort of ossified into the eccentric artistic bachelor, a role that has its erotic charms, I've discovered, to various women who pass through my life. But the pleasure of all this—and pleasure is, after all, supposedly my main motivation—hasn't held up over the years, not consistently anyway. At first I blamed the boredom, the sense of dissatisfaction I've been feeling more and more strongly over the past ten or fifteen years, simply on drinking too much alcohol. I'm no stranger to my Maine village's local AA meetings. But they've been a sort of revolving door to me: I'll get sick of the gray hungover mornings, the fact that Scotch and wine aren't acting as aphrodisiacs anymore, the fact that one more woman has told me I'm the most impossible and selfish man in the world, and I'll think, time to give up the booze again. I suppose I'm no different from a bowery bum who's been kicked in the head one too

many times and decides to go to his regular rehab for a hot meal and a cot, even if it means giving up booze to do it.

But sometimes I have experienced a deeper kind of momentary lift—stopping drinking, walking once again into that Methodist church basement for an AA meeting all constitute an *action,* something definite I'm doing to climb out of my gray rut. I feel for that moment like maybe I do have some control over my life, that maybe there *are* actions I can take to get me back on track. But then the meetings and the sobriety-speak and the absurdity of sitting down to a perfect French or Italian meal— I'm a gourmet cook, so this dilemma comes up a lot—without the perfect wine and, even more than that, the awkwardness of being with a woman without the lubrication of a good drink . . .

Well, it stops working, I mean sobriety stops working, and I begin to feel so much resentment over the deprivation of not being able to drink that I just can't keep it up. So I drink again. And it's *not* like what I hear a lot of AA old-timers say. I don't instantly turn into a hopeless wreck. I've never stopped painting—frankly, I think I've improved as a painter, whether or not I drink. My life doesn't fall apart completely. But I suppose something inside me is slowly wearing away, something that doesn't always show at the surface. At least, finally, after decades of this in-and-out stuff, with this woman Louise I've been involved with over the past six months, I'm discovering that more is going on in me, more is sort of *dying* in me, than I realized. And I'm more hurt and angry than I ever had a clue I was.

Louise, divorced and forty-five, moved to Lawrence's Maine town in the effort to get away from everything in her past life, especially her ex-husband. She was seeking, Lawrence said, "the kind of idyllic small-town experience that probably no longer exists anywhere, not while you can get MTV and the Playboy Channel even in the middle of the woods. But it was the classic thing of wanting to get away from it all, away from the hectic driven impersonal pace of New York City, where she'd lived all her married life, away from all the confusions and disappointments and unhappiness she'd known for decades before. She had enough money saved up and was getting enough alimony to plant herself here. She hoped to find a teaching position somewhere in the county eventually—she was qualified to teach junior and senior high— but she wanted to take a year or two off, as she put it, 'just to breathe.' While breathing, she ran into me."

The beginning of Lawrence and Louise's relationship mirrored every other relationship Lawrence had had.

I know I'm appealing to women, at least at the beginning. I'm so involved in my work, my painting, that I guess I come across as some kind of mythical creature— some driven romantic genius sequestering himself in the Maine woods—and that's an irresistible notion to most women I've met. Louise started out to be no exception. Well, there *was* something a little different about her. She never looked at me or my work entirely uncritically. She wouldn't, like most women I've known, simply stand in respectful silence in front of one of my canvases or ooh and aah on cue. She actually *looked* at my work. She asked questions about it. She asked me why I decided to use the composition I did. Why I chose the palette of color I did. She had a little experience herself of painting, so she was as interested in the technical details of my work as in the emotional. But I guess the strongest feeling I had from the start was that here was someone who wasn't blind, someone who actually had the power to *see* what I was doing—and, by extension, see more of who *I* really was. This unnerved me a little, but I had such confidence in my seductive abilities that I thought I could get around it.

Louise was—is—a very attractive woman. Very physical, slightly overripe, sensual body. I wanted to paint her, which I rarely want to do with people, women or not. Most of my work is land- and seascape stuff. But something about her sheer presence, the physicality of it, struck me. Over our first dinner, I told her this. She was shy about the idea of sitting for me and said she'd think about it. I knew then that she would probably think about everything before she agreed to do it, including lovemaking. This was no ordinary woman. It would take all the seductive skills I had to win her.

"Winning her" became a big motivation for Lawrence.

I'd met Louise during one of my sobriety stretches. I think I told myself I'd need all my wits to win this woman, that alcohol wouldn't help with this conquest—I know she was one of the reasons I didn't go back to drinking right off. My typical pattern is drinking for eight months to a year, a year and a half, quitting for six months or so, then back again. The pendulum had swung like that for nearly my whole adult life. But with Louise, I convinced myself I wouldn't start drinking again for a very long time. There was something about her that made me want to be fully *awake*. At first it was just that I wanted to get her into bed. That's always a primary rite of passage in any relationship—that's where I really feel I've won. But she wouldn't comply. She'd come for dinner as if granting me a favor—not snobbishly; it was just that she had a kind of dignity, and I guess a wariness, that made it seem like a triumph to get her to agree to anything.

I was so self-centered these first weeks, I imagined that it was all a seductive ruse on *her* part, like she was using various hard-to-get strategies on me. I imagined, in fact, that everything she did while she was with me was an attempt to manipulate me, just as I was attempting to manipulate her. It never occurred to me that she might be having feelings or thoughts that had nothing to do with me.

As the weeks grew into months, Lawrence's patience with what he thought of as "our simultaneous cat-and-mouse game" grew thin. "I think my inner drinking time clock was also ticking away, getting closer and closer to the 'drink again' alarm. In any event, I started to get moody with her when we'd spend time in my studio or over the dinner table—moody and restless and, I now realize, angry. Why was it taking so long to win this woman? Who did she think she was, anyway? Why was I wasting my time on winning her? Why was it so important to me? I finally brought things to a head over coffee—funny, it was cappuccino like what I've got in front of me now. I asked her right out what game she was playing with me. Why wouldn't she go to bed with me?"

Louise didn't at first say anything, Lawrence reports. "Then she looked me in the eye and said with great, even slowness, like this was something that had built up in her for a long time, something she'd thought about a great deal and now was finally the moment to articulate it: 'I don't go to bed with men who don't know anything about me.' I was shocked. Hadn't we spent nearly every weekend night talking, getting to know each other? Hadn't I let her into my life, my work? Hadn't I shown her how much I appreciated her critical eye and intelligence? How could she say I knew nothing about her?"

Lawrence shakes his head. "She was right, of course. The only topic we'd ever really talked about was me, my work, my life, my past. But I didn't put that together then, and she wasn't about to help me. She probably realized—correctly—that I wouldn't have gotten the message that I was as self-involved, self-centered as I was even if she'd gone through a long litany of evidence. She probably realized—again correctly—that I would have heard all that as if it were the same old criticism I'd always gotten from every other woman I'd known and that I'd chalk it up to some kind of 'hurt female' response that had nothing to do with me. So she said nothing more about the subject, thanked me for dinner, and said she had to go home."

Lawrence was dumbstruck—and angry.

I won't repeat the string of invective I started muttering to myself: *bitch* was the kindest word in it. But the general gist was "How dare she?" What really happened, of course, is that she touched a very sore button in me. And, as usual when sore buttons in me are touched, the only thing I could think to do was drink. I had a store of good Bordeaux still in the cellar. I'm now convinced that any alcoholic who keeps booze in his cellar, even if he's not drinking, is on some level *planning* to drink in the future—anyway, that's certainly true of me. I got out a bottle and a corkscrew and a wineglass and started the old descent into numbness. Wine always softened the edges before, always allowed me to rationalize my way out of any pain, get away from any sense of responsibility, I suppose. And it didn't let me down this time either. At least, as the alcohol began once again to seep into me, to do its softening stuff, I could allow myself to believe that Louise's dismissal of me was the product of her own neuroses in a way that I hadn't been able to do before sober. Once again I slid away from any feeling of guilt—that's the joy of wine, at least that was its greatest joy for me.

This began a familiar period of a work, drink, work, drink schedule for Lawrence.

However, past that first night of escape—it felt like an escape from Louise, but it was more an escape from myself—I couldn't drive out the message she'd given me. That I didn't know her—that I really hadn't known anybody—ever in my life. I was so self-absorbed, such a baby grabbing for quick gratification, that I hardly knew myself. I started to get paranoid. Maybe Louise knew me far better than I realized. Maybe her searching looks at my canvases had revealed something dark and horrible that only she knew. Of course she wouldn't want to go to bed with me! She'd discovered slowly, over the weeks, by being with me, listening to me, and above all seeing how my unconscious manifested all over my canvases, that I was a monster. I began to feel something I'd never felt before; it was as if I'd unleashed a self-loathing I'd never allowed myself to experience. And drinking wasn't keeping it at bay, not for long anyway. Finally, after about a week and a half of immersion in this alcohol-soaked self-loathing, I decided to call her. As it happens, I wasn't drunk when I picked up the phone—it was early morning, and as bad as I get, I don't drink in the mornings—not before ten-thirty or eleven A.M. anyway. But I'd had a horrible night, tossing and turning, dreaming of Louise appearing out of a dark mist, pointing at me, looking at me in that direct way of hers, accusing me of being an unspeakable monster . . .

Lawrence's first words to Louise when she picked up the phone were: "How could you do this to me? Why do you think I'm so horrible? What have I done to you?" Louise, Lawrence said, laughed a little. "It wasn't a guffaw, just a gentle little laugh, but I sure didn't appreciate it and I told her so. She apologized and suggested she come over for coffee and a talk. She did owe me an explanation, she said, and she did have something she wanted to say to me."

Louise came over and found a disheveled and nervous Lawrence at his kitchen table. "I was preparing myself for the worst, like a parent or a teacher was going to come in and let me have it. Louise sensed this, I think. I mean, she was gentle, and she smiled, and she caught me off guard by saying she hadn't come over to criticize me. She came over, she said, to talk about herself—not me."

For the first time, Louise let Lawrence know about the marriage she'd left, her life in New York, the wounds of this life and how raw and unhealed they still were. "Sometimes when you'd go on and on about this or that theory of art," Lawrence quotes her as saying,

I'd be a million miles away. You'd use an expression that my ex-husband often used—"you know what I mean?"—so often that it sort of ricocheted me out of the conversation and back to memories of the old terrible life in New York. My husband was—still is, I guess—a womanizing drunk. And I'm sorry, but you have all the earmarks of exactly the same thing. You have a lot more charm than he did and a lot more talent, and I guess I was willing to see if, maybe, your being an artist made you fundamentally different from my ex-husband. But, even though you never drank with me, it was still like being with him. I don't think there's anything more frustrating than being with someone as sealed off as he and you are. You sense that there's a spirit somewhere within, but you can't get at it, because the outer defenses are so strong and so self-serving that there isn't even a crack you can really look into. You wonder why I would peer for so long at your canvases. It was because I was trying to find you! I thought because you didn't drink that maybe there'd be a chance. I know from living with an active alcoholic, there simply isn't any chance—the drinking locks the soul up so tightly that nobody can get in. But everything about you was locked away. And I guess I started to get angry, because here I'd sent myself to the boondocks to get away from that horrible feeling of being locked out, and who do I find in the middle of the woods? You. And all you seem to see in me is a prize, a bed partner to be won, a conquest. Do you realize you've never once asked me about my life? About my feelings?

Lawrence says most of the above is a quote, but he can't help paraphrasing some of it.

I guess I'm giving it a slant that I felt it had underneath. I mean, I'm giving the impression that she was riding me, tearing me down, when really she wasn't. She was simply explaining how she felt. But I also heard the rest—or maybe I heard what I'd been trying to tell myself. Whether or not I drank, I had never really learned to be present. Not just to other people who of course, sooner or later, would see me as selfish and locked up, but *to myself*. I'd thought of drinking and sobriety as a kind of simple toggle switch you could turn on and off with various predictable results. When you drank, you could escape, you could soften the edges, you could rationalize your life to yourself. When you stopped drinking, you stopped having hangovers, but the romance, the softening, the ability to rationalize, was severely curtailed. Basically I was caught in a rut between the two because I'd already decided I knew everything about what each—drinking and not drinking—meant. Neither being drunk or being sober had enabled me to unlock myself, so both were very unsatisfying states, one neither better nor worse than the other. But Louise opened my eyes; perhaps I was just ready to have my eyes opened. *There were other people out there,* there was a self inside me I hadn't even begun to explore. There were, in other words, *presences* I hadn't begun to acknowledge existed or could exist.

Becoming sober and satisfied, Lawrence says, is a very different deal than simply deciding not to drink anymore.

I guess I'd been going through the motions of soul-searching in my painting, and Louise tells me that more is on my canvas than I realize, most particularly a feeling of being locked up—I'm a meticulous realist and consider every stroke of the brush very carefully before I'll let it touch the canvas. Frankly, as I began to let Louise's tone and message seep into me, I saw that I'd never allowed myself one spontaneous moment—not really. Everything was the product of an exacting control. My seductions, my paintings, my cooking, my home, even my attempts at sobriety. Not that there was anything wrong about control—you can't make a good soufflé or a good seascape without it—but when there is nothing else, when nothing *live* is allowed to come out, you're producing dead work. And my life had become a kind of dead work.

In the wake of all of this, Lawrence has made what he feels is not only a new commitment to sobriety, but a new commitment to becoming more involved in everything in his life—everything and everyone.

I feel like I'm starting from square one. Sometimes all this means is that I stop myself from talking when I feel the old urge to cover the silence with theory or rationalization. I've spent more time with Louise, for instance, just listening to her. I'm not so eager to get her or anyone else at the moment into bed either. It doesn't seem the kind of urgent prize or conquest it used to. God knows that might change as my old hormones start leaping about again. But, for now, I feel a kind of quiet and expectant peace, like, if I'll only hold still for long enough and simply listen to and look at what's around me, I'll get a few surprises. I've gone back to the occasional AA meeting, too, and don't feel the need I used to feel to wave my hand wildly to get called on. I don't need to break the silence the way I used to. I've no clue how long this new attitude will last or how it is going to change my life, I mean, I don't expect I'm going to leap into marriage with Louise (assuming she'd have me) or anyone else any time soon. I also don't know that I'll never drink again. But I want to keep this new attitude of seeing what's around me for as long as I can. I feel like I've been missing so much life these past decades. I want to jump off the pendulum I've been on and see what it's like to creep around on my own two feet in some new directions. I just have this idea there's a lot more territory to explore out there . . .

"I Know What's Sober for You, but What's Sober for Me?"

If we've gotten one message from everyone we've met in this book, it's that our paths to the kinds of awareness Lawrence talks about emerge for us very idiosyncratically: they fit who we are. Sobriety is not an interchangeable experience or state of being: what encourages open-eyed, playful sober consciousness in one person might send another person back, perhaps, to drugs and booze. No one's path to sobriety or maintaining sobriety is precisely the same as anyone else's.

The next story about a gay man in his midthirties named Mark is perhaps the most "heretical" in this book. I offer it neither to condemn nor condone the decisions Mark has made about achieving and sustaining his brand of consciousness. I offer it simply to report on yet another human being's reality—a reality that describes the bold outlines of experience of many people besides Mark. What is that experience? Basically, Mark gave up drinking and doing cocaine in some reasonably classic ways: he hit bottom, realized that booze and cocaine were killing him, and has made a day-to-day pact with himself not to drink or do coke again, a pact he has sustained now for twelve years with the support of friends, family, and therapy. The decision not to drink or do coke is very clear to him. As he puts it, "those are two lids I won't ever open again." But there's another lid Mark has decided to open. "Occasionally," he says, "I'll smoke pot."

No literature on recovery ever reports on the Marks of the world, and yet the experience Mark relates is by no means rare. The model of addiction as one from which we can only recover through strict abstinence is the model that dictates most of the literature you'll find on the bookshelves. But Mark's testimony at the very least asks us to inspect this idea, questioning its possible narrowness. I ask that you not judge Mark's testimony automatically or harshly either for or against it. I ask you simply to listen to him. And to consider the question he asks himself: "Am I relapsing? Or am I living my life in a way that's okay and even sober for me?"

After I stopped drinking and doing coke, it was clear to me that the disease I still had was self-hate. I've heard people talk about addiction or alcoholism as a disease of self-esteem, and I think that's doubly true of a lot of gay alcoholics and addicts. I don't mean to whine on like a helpless, hopeless victim—which, by the way, I don't think I am—but having a sexuality hated by much of the world in addition to ruining your life with drugs and alcohol doesn't exactly make you a happy camper. I know a lot of gay men who desperately mold their bodies into some Adonislike condition they hope will make them at least marginally acceptable. It's like we think we have to *wear* our bodies, like Armani suits: they're all we have, they're all anyone cares about. That and how much money we've got. Anyway, it's not news that gay people as a group don't have high rates of self-esteem. Both from within and without, both from our families and the general culture, we're not exactly embraced for our sexual proclivities.

I also come from a long line of drunks. My father and mother both are on the verge of drinking themselves to death; my brother and I all grew up as classic Children of Alcoholics. I've never liked AA or NA, they always seemed like a kind of religious indoctrination or something, but I have read some books about COAs, and I identify right down the line. You grow up thinking you've got to earn love and attention but you never know what *will* earn it. It's like something out of Kafka: you're told there are rules you must follow on pain of death, but you're not told what the rules are. And so you try to psych them out.

Mark makes a sound somewhere between a grumble and a laugh. "Good luck doing that. What gets a modicum of love and attention one day will get you smacked across the face the next. Life, for my brother and me, was hell."

The hell continued through Mark's own use and abuse of alcohol and cocaine. "There's not much to tell about that, except that after a couple of decades, they just didn't work anymore—they couldn't get me outside myself or, more accurately, outside my own self-loathing. All they were getting me was physically sick and paranoid." Mark stopped both one late morning after a trick he'd met at a bar left his apartment and he couldn't remember the guy's name or what they'd done in bed. "I felt like something loathsome, something you'd find under a rock, slimy and disgusting and completely worthless. I knew I had to stop wasting myself the way I was. I didn't know what life would be like without coke or booze, I only knew I couldn't do them anymore—I didn't *want* to do them anymore."

Mark's younger brother, Bob, was a godsend to him: "Something in me told me to call Bob, tell him I'd stopped drinking and drugging—I think I needed to actually *say* those words to somebody—and Bob almost wept when he heard it. Bob never touched alcohol or drugs, such was his fear of what they might do to him— he desperately didn't want to turn into our parents. He's got his own baggage about that, which he's working out in therapy. But I couldn't have found anyone more supportive. Through him and friends of his—both straight and gay, by the way (Bob's straight, but he knows a lot of different people, and he doesn't give a damn who you go to bed with)—I began to connect with people who weren't just out to get high, get laid, and get away from their own very poor self-views. Eventually I got into therapy myself and began to ask—very tentatively, I can tell you!—some basic questions about who I was, what I wanted to do and be."

Mark says that the past twelve years have had their rocky emotional moments, but he feels, bit by bit, "like I've discovered a self and I'm having a life. My life no longer seems like some bad mistake, something totally dependent on a malevolent fate. I know I have power now, power to direct myself wherever I want to go. I've gone back to music school—at one point in my beleaguered childhood, I was a pretty good pianist—and I'm discovering that my talent hasn't gone away. This is giving me a vent I've grown to depend on more and more; it teaches me that there are many ways of releasing what's inside of me, many ways of getting who I am out into the world." Recently, Mark took a vacation at a friend's house in Oregon, deep in the woods—no electricity, you had to carry water in buckets up from a well, the great outdoors was your bathroom, the whole living-in-the-wilds deal.

My friend is a superannuated hippie, I guess. I mean, he's in his midforties, got married on top of a mountain somewhere in northern California, and has been following a number of Buddhist and Native American practices that he says "ground" him. The other thing is, he likes the occasional toke of marijuana. He'd invited several

people to his cabin besides me, and after a vegetarian
meal of some kind of surprisingly tasty squash and
potato stew, he suggested we all light up a joint. I was sitting next to a woman who visibly tensed—I didn't know
until later that she was an ardent AA-goer, and the
prospect of being even in the presence of marijuana
smoke made her nervous. But, again, I didn't know this
until later, and whatever she was feeling didn't stop her
from taking some tokes off the joint. It was mild stuff,
very pleasant, and although I had some qualms about in-
haling it as it was passed around, I wasn't really all that
freaked out by it. But this woman, Alison, was. She got
up abruptly from the group and said she had to go out
and get some air. Something in me made me want to go
out after her. I didn't know what I wanted to do or say, I
just saw that she was really upset and I didn't want her to
be alone. I found her sitting on a fallen log outside the
door. I sat down next to her.

She was sobbing: "How could I have done that? I've
just shot seven years of sobriety to hell! Now I'll have to
go back to my AA meeting and confess this and start
counting days all over again. Why did I do it? Why did I
let myself *do* it?" She went on like this for a while, and I
was struck by her pain—the terror, really, she was obviously feeling, probably in no way helped by the effects of
the pot she'd just smoked.

I didn't say anything, I didn't try to talk her out of her
distress, I just sat there next to her and marveled that I
didn't feel the way she did. I know I don't have the kind
of pressure that going religiously to AA or NA can make
you feel. I didn't have to confess anything to anyone. I
didn't have to "count days" and "start" sobriety all over.
I guess that was the feeling—that there was no horrible
pressure on me to do anything. Somehow, over the past

twelve years, an inner sense of myself had strengthened to the point where I knew I could survive certain forays into territory that Alison thought of as taboo. Again, even feeling the effects of pot, I was clear that the experience I'd had with cocaine and drinking were murderous and that I truly did not want to experiment with that side of things ever again. But smoking this joint hadn't destroyed me.

Afterward, days afterward, I didn't crave pot. It occurred to me that, at a party, I could probably indulge in it if I wanted to, but I didn't feel I *needed* to. Okay, maybe this is a story that still has to pan out. Maybe I just haven't gotten to the point of needing it yet. Maybe this is all lying to myself. Maybe the insidious roots of addiction have been planted in me already, and I don't realize how overwhelmed I'll eventually be by them. But I already have such a strong network of people whom I talk to about everything, from my brother to my therapist to various close friends, I already have so many built-in crap detectors, really—people who will tell me if they think I'm kidding myself—that I *feel* like I'm being honest. I mean, I'm not trying to hide what I do from anyone. Who else is it affecting anyway?

I guess the most liberating thing about allowing myself to smoke marijuana occasionally is that it just reinforces the *individual* path I'm taking in my life. Nobody else knows what it is like to be me, what I can tolerate, what I can't, what I love, what I don't. And I have to say, I've been with many, many Twelve-Steppers who will do the occasional snort of 'poppers'—amyl nitrate—during sex, which I'll sometimes do as well. Poppers, from what I've read about them, seem to be relatively harmless, and their effects are fleeting. But I'm not here to sell anyone on pot or poppers or, for that matter, the more legitimate prescribed medications that many Twelve-Step people also take, that menu of antidepressants that ranges from Prozac to Zoloft to Xanax. All I'm discovering for myself is what *I* can and can't or don't want to do. As long as I stay honest, as long as I keep talking about the decisions I make, including my fears and ambivalences about them, I feel like I'm on the larger right track.

Is Mark deluding himself? Perhaps that's a question only he can answer. Calling someone else an addict does nothing for the person in question other than categorize him or her in *your* mind. Calling someone else sober is just as useless an endeavor. We don't *know* what anyone else needs, feels, is capable of without self-destruction. Simply not drinking doesn't seem to be enough on its own to constitute sobriety. Witness Lawrence, who, though occasionally abstinent, was miserable and far from sober in any sense of leading a self-accepting or sat-isfied life. But I don't rush to defend Mark; again, I only offer his experience for you to draw what conclusions you will from it. Perhaps your experience is not so differ-ent from his. At the very least, you'll see that you're not alone in that experience. What you *do* next about it— well, once again, that depends on you, your needs, de-sires, fears.

Mark does hint at an important element in making whatever decisions we make: self-honesty. He has a net-work of people he can talk to about whatever he does in his life. This, in his and my and so many other people's experience, is a crucial part of learning to live con-sciously: finding various sounding boards we can trust to mirror back to us what we're doing, saying, feeling, thinking. At that point, you can decide if you're pushing closer to life or to death, to consciousness or the fearful escape from consciousness.

Blanketing the Loss of a Baby

At various points in her life, had you asked her about her use of marijuana and consumption of alcohol, Janice would have given you a story not unlike Mark's. "I can handle it," would have been her theme. "I know what I'm doing. I have control over it. It just relaxes me, helps me to enjoy life more." But recently, Janice's reflections on her frequent returns to smoking pot and drinking have led her to some new acknowledgments. The simplest of them is this: "Why do I keep *having* to return to pot and alcohol? I mean, if they were no problem, why do I keep trying to *quit* them?"

Janice has finally found out more about the feelings that have urged her into these swings back and forth. "I know it goes back to my childhood—my first teen years. I know now that there's a loss I'm still grappling with, a loss I thought I'd put behind me." Janice had a child when she was thirteen, a child "everyone quickly agreed," she said, "should be put up for adoption." Janice is now twenty-eight.

I guess I started to question my roller-coaster experience of drinking and drugging when I realized that my daughter is now two years older than I was when I had her. What I realized is that I've never gotten over losing her. There's been a kind of tension in me for all these years that hasn't let up for a moment, not really. I mean, I don't walk around tearing my hair out. I got my life pretty much back into order after she was born. I went to college, did all the right stuff. It was easy to rationalize my way back to normal life: how could I have taken care of a little baby when I was a child myself? I would have ruined both of our lives. But I still feel like something was ripped out of me—literally and figuratively. It's like a part of myself I didn't realize I needed but now feel the loss of every moment of my life. And, until recently anyway, drinking and smoking pot helped me to deaden those feelings, get away from them.

Janice became a social worker and found herself working with—"actually, I see now that subconsciously I was always looking for"—unwed mothers who decided to keep their kids, helping them get whatever benefits were due them, counseling them emotionally, aiding them in ways that make her feel like she's helping the mother she might have been. "It's very difficult but sometimes satisfying work," Janice says.

I just never realized until recently that I'd never really looked at the feelings that kept me so bound to this job. They seem so obvious now, but I can't tell you how I blinded myself to them. It's like I'm working out my own pain over the loss of my daughter through my association with every woman I work with. My boyfriend is the one who finally got me to see this. Calvin is black and a pretty militant activist, not only about racial stuff, but about the environment, American imperialism—you name it. I've been with him for five years now. He seems to deal with his anger through his work as directly as I deal with my sorrow through mine. He's just more aware that's what he's doing. What he also got aware of is that my drinking and smoking dope were getting out of control. Calvin isn't an addictive personality at all. I mean, he can take it or leave it. So when I'd drink some wine or light up a joint, he'd sometimes have a little, too. But he'd stop when it made him dizzy or when he was really interested in something else, like a book or a program on television he absolutely had to see, and he'd just forget to finish the joint or the glass of wine. It just wasn't important to him.

I can't *imagine* not finishing a joint or a glass of wine. I used to joke, "Think of all those Mormons in Salt Lake City! How desperately *they* need to get high! How could I pass up a joint thinking how much they needed it?" A sort of twist on all the starving children in India . . . Anyway, Calvin would just look at me as if I were nuts. Why did I have to consume so much? What was going on? He really didn't understand what a craving for alcohol or drugs was like. And I tried to model myself on him. I mean, I would give up drinking and smoking dope for "health" reasons—I'd go on some purist diet that banned all foreign substances, and Calvin would tag along, curious about the effects of the diet—and I'd convince myself I was as laid back as he was. I didn't *need* to drink or smoke. I could give it up any time I wanted to. But it never lasted long. I went back and forth, back and forth. And the swings back into drugs and alcohol were catching Calvin's attention. I was beginning to lose it. I'd go all numb, be totally silent, and then just start to cry quietly. This would happen again and again. Calvin didn't understand. What was wrong with me? What great sadness was in me that seemed to come out without my knowing anything about it?

It was when Janice found herself counseling a client at work who had gotten pregnant again and was debating whether or not to get an abortion that Janice's own motives became clearer to her.

I listened to this woman as she described the squalor of her life—no husband, oldest kid hooked on crack, babies screaming—sometimes she couldn't help but hit

them, they drove her so nuts, her mother acting as baby-
sitter but getting drunk on rotgut wine . . . She went on
with this horror story, but all I could think of was the little being growing in her womb. And it hit me, by stages,
deeper and deeper, just how horribly alone and sad I felt
about my own baby. It hit me at that moment that I'd
turned to any escape I could find to get away from this
sorrow, but I couldn't get away from it anymore. It was
just there, in me, as definite a fact as the fetus growing in
the womb of the woman who was crying about her miserable life right now in front of me.

"There's another part of this," Janice says.

My mother was always a very quiet and depressed
woman. When she found out about my pregnancy and
made the arrangements for the adoption, she barely
talked to me about it. I guess I felt like, slowly, I was turning into my mother—drying up, keeping it all inside.
Strangely, what alcohol and pot were doing to me was to
numb me and then somehow carve out a channel for my
sadness, which would then come out of me just like it
had for my mother. I can't tell you the number of times
I'd come home from school and find my mother sitting
at the kitchen table crying softly. Whatever great sadness
was in her was also in me. I'm now going to a therapist,
and she's suggested that the baby I gave up for adoption
is sort of like the "me" I gave up, somehow, at the same
time. It's a symbol of life I feel I gave away—my own life.
I mean, I'm also curious about my daughter, what she's
like—I ache sometimes so much to see her—but I see
that's symbolic, too.

    All I can say is, when I got home from that session
with the poor overwrought pregnant woman, something

had released in me, some realization that I still did have a life, I hadn't given it away, and I didn't have to become the depressed vacant woman my mother was. Some tiny feeling of courage seeped in, the courage to breathe more freely, take some risks to *live* more freely. It was like I discovered a kind of life force inside me that alcohol and pot had always just deadened or, recently, channeled into sadness. I felt like I'd gotten off a merry-go-round: there wasn't going to be a *need* now to escape through wine and pot.

Through therapy, I've strengthened this feeling. I've even made it somewhat comprehensible to Calvin. He may not be an addict, but he is a human being, and he struggles with the expression of his own life force. Sobriety now seems like a matter of unclogging an air hose: I don't want to distort everything with drugs and booze anymore. I want to *breathe* without any blockage. I want to reclaim the life I gave up when I gave up my daughter.

The Pull Between Life and Death

Considering what leads to slips or relapses or even new definitions of what they are is really a continuation of the discussion we've been having throughout this book. What impedes us from living freely, passionately? How do we define these impediments, understand them, get out from under their weight, or even dissolve them? We're grappling with more than sobriety or addiction as we consider these questions. We're grappling with the very forces of life and death.

Freud identified two giant, imperial urges of which alcoholics and addicts give perhaps the most dramatic evidence: the libidinal life drive and the aggressive death drive. They pummel and provoke us both to create and to destroy. At the best times we're able to wed these seemingly contradictory drives so that they serve us. In fact, nothing positive can be achieved *without* an aggressive force serving a libidinal aim. We're not only driven by both urges, we need both. One, the libidinal, gives us a life-affirming goal; the other, the aggressive, gives the strength and/or genuine wrath it takes to achieve that goal.

But sometimes—witness the hell of our addictive lives—the aggressive force gets the upper hand and turns against us. We have, in our own lives, powerful evidence of two contradictory facts:

1. Alcohol and drugs allowed us to check out in sometimes magically effective, transcendent, and even soul-satisfying ways.
2. Alcohol and drugs brought us to unprecedented depths of self-destruction, lifelessness, and misery.

Both these facts are true, but what fuels anybody's motivation to stop drinking or drugging is the fact that the latter fact has proved to be truer: it's only when misery becomes the more reliable outcome of drinking and drugging than transcendence that we start to yearn to stop. It's only when the death drive is allowed to reign unchecked and unchanneled that we come to crave the life drive. This is the beginning of the urgent desire for consciousness, for sobriety. We decide we want to live more than die.

But sometimes we're just too terrified to reroute, to choose a more libidinal aim. Sometimes the known hell as well as the known rewards of self-destruction seem to be the only realm we know or can trust. The blast of sobriety, the inescapable *light* of it, a light that may suddenly reveal what may look like the chaos and unpredictability of our lives and personalities, can fill us with a desperation and hopelessness so strong that we long once again for the "dark" of getting drunk or high. And so we slip. We make a desperate dive back into the dark sea whose monsters we know well, but whose soporific comforts are the only ones we feel we can trust. Unfortunately, the monsters soon outnumber the comforts: we long to gasp for air. But where is the "air" we can breathe? It may not seem to be anywhere. We've tried sobriety; we've tried drugs and alcohol. We may get to a point where we don't believe that either realm can offer us any solace. This desperation can become suicidal. I know many men and women who *have* killed themselves because neither sobriety nor drugs or alcohol seemed to offer any avenue of escape; the only course seemed to be to abandon life altogether.

There *is* a way through this terrible suicidal bind and blackness. When you finally let go of the rope in the tug of war between sobriety and addiction, what you often find is that your desperation was misplaced. There is a softer, wider, profoundly more comforting consciousness awaiting you when you're able to relax your fierce grip—either on being sober or drinking and drugging. Once again the profoundly healing realization is that *you've got options.* You've seen that our goal as sober people isn't to chastise ourselves into behaving because we are or have been bad or forcing ourselves into any other stricture of right and wrong. It's to find a way to pursue passionate and fulfilling lives without killing ourselves. You've seen that our range of options is always larger, infinitely larger, than we once allowed ourselves to believe it could be.

This gives you focus: to sort out death from life in the

choices you make and to understand that you can experience more pleasure and fulfillment choosing life than
choosing death. However, nobody is going to slap your
hand: you already know that you can pick up a drink or
a drug any time you want to. Nobody has any power to
stop you from doing that as you've proven to yourself
again and again. Nobody has the power to get you to
stop drinking or drugging either. It is your own exercise
of choice that determines what you do.

The most effective choices we make seem to be those
we make *for ourselves,* not for what we imagine are
other people's expectations or requirements of us. As
you've seen in all the stories in these pages, it doesn't
seem to matter what realm of recovery these choices lead
you to—AA, therapy, turning to family and friends,
winging it on your own. But if you get no other message
from this chapter and this book than that you can
choose, in fact right now *are choosing,* your own path,
our time together has been a success. I have no desire to
stop you from doing anything or to coerce you into doing anything you don't want to do. What I can offer you
is what I have offered you: stories of men and women
who feel what you're feeling—the eternal tug between
life and death, the inescapable ambivalence not only of
grappling with addictions but of being human, an ambivalence that, when we give ourselves the opportunity
truly to look at it, presents us, moment to moment, with
an extensive menu of choices.

Just *see* that menu: this is the first step toward choosing something on it that won't hammer you into unconsciousness. You'll find any number of choices that
promise you pleasure and nourishment and an unprecedented feast of life.

Index